happy belly

BREAKWATER
P.O. Box 2188, St. John's, NL, Canada, A1C 6E6
WWW.BREAKWATERBOOKS.COM

A CIP catalogue record for this book is available from Library and Archives Canada.

Copyright © 2022 Aaron McInnis

ISBN 978-1-55081-921-2

We acknowledge the financial support of the Government of Canada and the Government of Newfoundland and Labrador through the Department of Tourism, Culture, Industry and Innovation for our publishing activities.

PRINTED AND BOUND IN CANADA.

Breakwater Books is committed to choosing papers and materials for our books that help to protect our environment. To this end, this book is printed on a recycled paper that is certified by the Forest Stewardship Council®.

MAN VERSUS CAKE

PRESENTS

happy belly

The Cake Book

WRITTEN BY **Aaron McInnis**

PHOTOGRAPHED BY
Aimee Nicole Photography

BREAKWATER

CONTENTS

FOREWORD • 7

PREFACE • 9

ACKNOWLEDGEMENTS • 10

MAN BEHIND THE CAKE • 13

CAKER 101: TIPS AND TECHNIQUES • 15

TOOLS • 24

CONVERSION TABLE AND SCOOP TABLE • 25

STANDARD RECIPES • 27

CANDY BAR COLLECTION • 45

CLASSIC DESSERTS, REIMAGINED • 67

CLASSIC PAIRINGS • 91

HOLIDAY AND CELEBRATION CAKES • 117

OUT-OF-THE-BOX FLAVOUR PAIRINGS • 147

SEASONAL FLAVOURS • 169

INDEX • 201

FOREWORD

CAKE . . . AAHHHH, CAKE!

Done right, it's like a hug on the inside. A time machine to memories of days past, and a vehicle for new memories in the making. Old-school, home-made cakes can't be replaced by fancy-pants, only-for-Instagram desserts. Cake done right is what close-your-eyes-good moments are made of. Aaron gets this. He understands that love and hard work and beautifully simple ingredients are really all you need to make yourself happy.

In this book, Aaron has brilliantly distilled a vast number of recipes down to a few foundational ones, and gives the home baker a simple roadmap for successful and stunning cakes and cupcakes. He gives you permission not only to follow the map but also to go off-roading with your own spin on his core recipes.

This is a fun, easy, and inspirational cookbook from an equally inspirational guy. He pours passion and love into everything he does and it shows in these pages.

KIMBERLY BAILEY
Food Network Judge | Chief Cake Artist and Chief Cake Officer,
The Butter End Cakery

Kimberly Bailey is the award-winning cake artist and Chief Cake Officer of the Butter End Cakery in Los Angeles. Her culinary art was incubated in a one-room guest house in Venice, California, while she was recovering from her first bout of cancer. Ten years later, she is a familiar judge on Food Network on shows including *Buddy vs. Duff 2*, *Wedding Cake Championship*, *Winner Cake All*, and others. In her studio, Kimberly and her team have been featured on two seasons of *Ridiculous Cakes*. She has been awarded Best Wedding Cake Artist in Los Angeles multiple times by California Wedding Day and listed as one of the top 60 pastry pros in America by Martha Stewart. Her work has been featured in every major wedding publication, blog, and entertainment magazine.

PREFACE

"LIFE'S TOO SHORT TO SAY NO TO CAKE."

Which is exactly why, as *Man versus Cake*, I bring you *Happy Belly—The Cake Book.*

There is something to be said for having a collection of recipes as large as the library, but my question is why? Do you truly need every one of those torn-out magazine pages, scraps of paper, and church-fundraiser cookbooks? I wholeheartedly believe that with the right foundation recipes, you have a world of possibilities staring right back at you.

Although baking is a science, it takes passion, desire . . . and yes, the secret ingredient, love, to make a recipe come together. Okay, a tried-and-true recipe does help kick-start the process.

In this book, I will share the recipes that built me, the recipes that I used to build my business. I will show you how to take my basic recipes and make countless new cake combinations. We don't need fifty different cake recipes; we just need one and an imagination and desire to create something delicious.

You can't always bake a cake recipe into cupcakes, but with the foundation recipes in this book, you can. You can bake these recipes into either cakes or cupcakes!

Everything found in this book was created as you see it. Every cake was assembled as described and tested!

Be the baker you always knew you could be, and impress even the toughest of critics with a simply delicious moist cake. They will swoon over the taste and the incredible appearance!

However, if you're not careful, you'll be expected to bring dessert to every get-together from now on.

ACKNOWLEDGEMENTS

PEOPLE ASK ME WHY I DO THIS, AND FOR ME, THE ROOT OF IT ALL IS ALWAYS MY FAMILY.

If it weren't for my wife and children, would I honestly dig as deep as I do, work as hard as I do, and strive to be the best version of me? I know me, and the answer is no. No, I wouldn't. I want my children to see that you will have to put in the effort and be your best you.

Melissa, thank you. Thank you for being there no matter what, every late night, every early morning, every delivery, every pickup, every far-fetched idea and every failure. Your endless support and infinite love are undeserved on the best of days, but I am thankful and truly blessed to be your husband. God placed you in my life exactly when you were needed; His blessings have found us on so many occasions.

To my sons, Nathan, Kingston, and Owen, of all the roles I play, being your dad will always be my favourite. The three of you give me purpose. You may not see that, but one day I pray you will understand it for yourselves.

There are so many people to thank who helped me along the road to where I am now, and I could write a book about them all. So to my family and friends: you are deeply cared about, and I thank God each day for placing you in my life.

I may be full of the ideas, the recipes, and creation of the cakes themselves, but Aimee Power's keen eye and stunning photographs bring the cakes to life. Working with Aimee was nothing short of a pleasure. She was full of patience and exuded kindness. Her attention to the smallest details and her willingness, passion, and dedication put me at ease. I knew my cakes and photos were in great hands. Aimee, this book was a dream for me, and it was so easy to trust you with it.

◀ Aimee Power
ww.facebook.com/aimeenicolephotos • aimeenicolephotography.com
709-334-2642

MAN
BEHIND
THE CAKE

MY NAME IS AARON MCINNIS, BORN AND RAISED IN NOVA SCOTIA AND A NEWFOUNDLAND TRANSPLANT SINCE 2005, WHEN I BEGAN MY JOURNEY THROUGH UNIVERSITY.

I am the owner of Happy Belly Cakery, the custom cake studio, and *Man versus Cake*, the international education blog. I've been baking for nearly all my life as a self-taught/mom-taught baker.

I strongly and wholeheartedly believe in breaking the cake stereotypes and empowering men to get into the kitchen to cake all the things. I am the father to three young men and I want them to know and understand that they belong wherever they find themselves most happy, making and creating a successful life for themselves and their family.

Some fun facts . . .

▶ I am a **CERTIFIED NUTRITIONIST**. I completed my bachelor's degree with a major in nutrition.

▶ I am one of only a handful of **RED SEAL CERTIFIED** bakers in Newfoundland.

▶ I am currently the Baking and Pastry Arts **INSTRUCTOR** with College of the North Atlantic in Newfoundland.

▶ I am a four-time **FOOD NETWORK VETERAN AND CHAMPION**, having competed in the following programs: *Spring Baking Championship*, Season 4: Top 5 | *Christmas Cookie Challenge*, Season 2, Episode 4: Winner | *Winner Cake All*, Season 1, Episode 1: Runner-Up | *The Big Bake*, Season 1, Episode 2: Runner-Up.

What it all boils down to in the end is that my passion has pushed me, my intrigue has taught me, my eagerness has helped me, and God has led me.

Grab your apron and your whisk and join me in the kitchen.

CAKER

101

TIPS AND TECHNIQUES

These tips and techniques can all be found on my YouTube channel: **www.youtube.com/manversuscake**.

CORING AND FILLING CUPCAKES

You can buy fancy cupcake corers that cost more than you really need to spend. My favourite tool to use for this is an apple corer. I have them in two sizes, both found from local dollar stores.

→   Remove enough of the cupcake to put a filling inside. I don't typically put the top back on because the buttercream will hide the hole. Bonus for the cake maker: eat the core!

→   Put the fillings into piping bags and simply cut a hole in the piping bag. When I am using caramel or liquid ganache, I use a squeeze bottle with a nozzle top rather than a piping bag; this allows me to gently warm it in the microwave if needed.

DAMMING AND FILLING A CAKE

Damming a cake is required when you have a filling that is not completely firm, for example, custards and curds. Even when chilled, they don't fully set. The dam around the edge of the cake creates a firm barrier for the filling.

→   Place buttercream or ganache into a piping bag, either with no tip or a 1A tip.

→   Pipe a solid line of frosting around the outer edge of the cake layer and then place a dollop in the centre of the layer as well. This helps when the cake is sliced up.

→   Fill the space between the outer edge and the centre dollop with the soft filling.

CREATING A DAM

Once trimmed, cake tops make great snacks: freeze for cake pops or use in trifles or other desserts.

LEVELLING

Levelling refers to trimming the dome top off a cake. Make the top flat so that you can layer the cakes easily. Follow the same guidelines as in *Torting*.

TORTING

Torting a cake refers to cutting the cake into multiple layers, horizontal to the cake plate.

→ Keep the knife hand still; the other hand does all the movement (the turning hand).

→ Place the cake on a turntable. With your knife hand, place the knife against the cake where you would like to cut. *Do not saw the cake.*

→ With the other hand, and tucking your elbow in tightly to your body to ensure an even cut, turn the cake. The sharp blade will easily and evenly glide through the cake, giving you a perfect cut.

SIMPLE SYRUP SOAK

Once cakes have been torted, squirt simple syrup from a squirt bottle (or use a pastry brush to apply a heavy layer of syrup) evenly over all layers of cake.

FROSTING FINISHES

NAKED CAKE

Naked cakes have *no* frosting or ganache on the outside of the cake. A naked cake will often have decorative dams piped during the layering process.

CRUMB COATING

A crumb coat is important for a perfect finish. It's a thin layer of buttercream or other frosting that traps any loose cake crumbs into it, and once set keeps them out of the final coat of frosting. It's a very important step that should *not* be skipped. The crumb coat is like the cake's container; it holds everything in.

SEMI-NAKED CAKE

If the cake has a *thin* crumb coat, then it's semi-naked. Some of the cake is still peeking through, but it's not as bare as a naked cake.

ROUGH OR RUSTIC BUTTERCREAM/GANACHE

When adding the final coat of buttercream, don't be as careful as for a smooth finish. Just be sure there is an even amount of frosting around the cake.

→ Smooth the frosting out very casually with a bench scraper, and then go back with the angled spatula to create the texture.

SMOOTH BUTTERCREAM/GANACHE

This is one of the most common finishes on a cake. For dessert-style cakes, don't spend a lot of time smoothing them out, because decorations tend to help cover things. And some slight imperfections add character.

For a smooth finish, make sure the butter-cream is a good consistency. It needs to spread easily and smoothly—a peanut-butter consistency or slightly thicker. Adjust this in American Butter-cream (page 33) by simply adding liquid, a little at a time.

→ With an offset spatula, apply frosting to the sides and top of the cake. Place the edge of a stainless-steel bench scraper against the butter-cream while resting the bottom on the turntable. The ninety-degree angle of the scraper will help achieve straight sides.

→ Holding the scraper in place, rotate the turntable with the other hand. Frosting will naturally smooth out in this motion; when you get back to where you started, scrape any excess buttercream back into the bowl. If the buttercream has any large imperfections, add a little more with the offset spatula and repeat the scraping process.

→ Once the sides are to your liking, take the scraper and turn it on its side. Hold it with four fingers on one side and your thumb on the other. Starting at the outer edge of the cake, drag the top lip inward towards the centre of the cake. Repeat this all the way around the top of the cake.

It doesn't take a lot of pressure to smooth either the sides or the top, just a little practice.

APPLYING SMOOTH BUTTERCREAM

CREATING A DRIP: BOWL AND SPOON METHOD

DRIPPING

Add as many or as few drips as you wish. The harder you squeeze, the further the drip will flow, so squeeze with different pressures to allow for variety on the cake.

→ While rotating the turntable, gently squeeze the bottle with the warm ganache or caramel sauce at the top edge of the cake, allowing the liquid to flow down the side.

The same results can be achieved using a bowl and spoon: carefully spoon different amounts of your drip over the side edge of the cake.

TEXTURED LINES

The lines can go in any direction, depending on the look you are trying to achieve for the cake.

→ Frost the cake with a smooth(ish) finish. But don't worry about it being perfect. Work with some speed, as you don't want a crust to form on the buttercream; it makes the process a little harder.

→ Take an offset spatula and hold the tip of it at an angle in the butter-cream. Depending on the lines you are looking to achieve, the next step will vary.

For vertical or diagonal lines, start from the bottom of the cake and gently drag the spatula through the buttercream in the direction you are looking for. Clean the spatula after each line and repeat.

For horizontal stripes, hold the spatula in one place and turn the turntable with your other hand. Stop and scrape the frosting off the spatula when you get back around to where you started. Move the spatula up a row and repeat all the way to the top.

If the buttercream forms a crust or the ganache is a little too set to make deep-enough indents: Boil some water and place it in a cup next to you. Warm the spatula and dry it off before creating the lines. The heat will soften the frosting and allow you to create texture.

PIPING TECHNIQUES

FILLING A PIPING BAG

Generally, people place their piping bag in a large glass to fill it. This process isn't as simple as it looks.

Instead, try folding the bag down over your non-dominant hand, creating a cup shape with your hand so that the pointed end of the bag is in your palm and the rest of the bag is folded down over the back of your hand.

When filling the bag, press the frosting into the bag to remove any large air pockets. Use your thumb as a stiff surface to scrape the spatula against.

For Cakes

Rosette Piping • Rosette piping is a beautiful and quick way to create a lot of texture on the side of the cake.

→ Place the buttercream in a piping bag with a 1M tip. You will get three to four rows, depending on the height of the stacked cake. I usually use my cake layers as a guide.

→ Hold the piping bag straight out from the cake, with the open part of the tip perpendicular to the side of the cake. Start in the middle of the cake layer, and with constant pressure begin piping in a circular motion. When you make one round, drag the "tail" of the rosette over to the side, where the next rosette will cover it.

ROSETTE PIPING

→ Repeat this process all the way around the cake until you get back to where you started.

→ On the next row, you want to offset the rosettes so that the centre of each one starts in the middle of the two rosettes below it, also making sure you are starting in the middle of that cake layer. Repeat the rosettes all the way around the cake. Make as many rows as necessary to reach the top of the cake.

→ Make rosettes in the same way across the top of the cake, working from the outside edge into the middle.

Petal Piping • Be warned . . . This technique is the most time-consuming of all the techniques: although impressive, it takes *a lot* of work.

→ Place buttercream in a bag with a 1A tip.

→ Hold the piping bag straight out from the cake with the open part of the tip perpendicular to the side of the cake. Pipe a line of buttercream dollops vertically up the side of the cake. Make sure each dollop touches the previous one.

→ With an offset spatula, squish the centre of the buttercream dollop and drag it to the right. Repeat this with each one.

→ Pipe the next set of dollops vertically up the cake over top of the tail of the previous one.

→ Repeat these same two steps over and over until you make it the entire way around the cake . . . it'll take a while.

→ On the last row of dollops, you won't really be able to drag the tails, so just gently squish them in, but be careful not to damage the row you started with.

For Cupcakes

6B Piping Tip • This piping tip can be used in place of either the 1M or the 1A tips to give the cupcakes a different look and texture.

1M Rosette • Hold the piping bag so that the open part of the tip is pointing down towards the top of the cupcake. Start in the centre of the cupcake and squeeze the bag with constant pressure while moving in a circular motion around the cupcake. You end up with a single layer of frosting all over the top of the cupcake.

1M or 1A Semi-Swirl • Start with a rosette, but instead of stopping when you reach the beginning, go around the cupcake a second time on top of the first layer of buttercream, and make this round slightly smaller. Stop when you get to where you started the second layer.

1M Classic Swirl • For the 1M classic swirl, repeat the steps of the semi-swirl but instead of stopping at the second row, continue to the third layer of buttercream. This layer is significantly smaller than the first and usually ends in a point.

1M Nest • A nest of buttercream is typically created on a cupcake that has a filling, *not* inside the cupcake itself, so it's similar to creating a dam on a cake.

Hold the piping bag as for a rosette, but instead of starting in the centre of the cupcake, you pipe just a border around the outside edge of the cupcake. You can pipe two layers if you wish.

1M Star Piping • Star piping is simply creating star- or flower-shaped dollops with the 1M tip. This technique is used to mimic hydrangea flowers. Hold the piping bag so that the open part of the tip is pointing down towards the top of the cupcake. Squeeze the piping bag and release pressure, thus dropping a star onto the cupcake. Repeat the process until cake is completely covered. You can add a second layer if you wish, for height and dimension.

1A High Top • A high-top cupcake is the same process as for a swirl. Pipe in one continuous motion with constant pressure until you reach as high as you want to go, releasing pressure at the very top to leave a point on the cupcake.

1A Blob • This one may have a technical name, but I don't know it! Hold the piping bag so that the open part of the tip is pointing down towards the top of the cupcake and about one to two inches away from the top. Start squeezing the piping bag with constant pressure. The buttercream will start to pool and create a large mound of frosting on top of the cupcake. Stop when you are happy with the amount.

The beauty of decorating cupcakes is that you can easily take the buttercream off and reuse it if you are unhappy with the piping.

There is no right or wrong piping tip to use to decorate a cupcake; it all boils down to the look you want to achieve. You can ultimately use the same motions with any piping tip in the bag.

CUPCAKE PIPING TECHNIQUES

6B Piping Tip – Classic Swirl

1M Piping Tip – Rosette

1A Piping Tip – Blob

1A Piping Tip – High Top

TOOLS

These tools will help make your baking and decorating more efficient and polished.

- apple corer
- immersion blender
- measuring cups/spoons
- offset spatulas
- pans
- parchment paper
- pastry brush
- piping bags, including tips/couplers
- rubber spatulas
- scoops (varying sizes)
- scrapers, kitchen
- silicone baking mats
- squeeze bottles
- stand mixer (for a few of the recipes)
- turntable

note When the recipes in this book call for milk, it's best to use 2% or whole milk.

CONVERSION TABLE

🥄	🥄	C	OZ
1 Tbsp	3 tsp	1/16 cup	1/2 ounce
2 Tbsp	6 tsp	1/8 cup	1 ounce
4 Tbsp	12 tsp	1/4 cup	2 ounces
5 + 1/3 Tbsp	16 tsp	1/3 cup	2 + 2/3 ounces
8 Tbsp	24 tsp	1/2 cup	4 ounces
10 + 2/3 Tbsp	32 tsp	2/3 cup	5 + 1/2 ounces
12 Tbsp	36 tsp	3/4 cup	6 ounces
16 Tbsp	48 tsp	1 cup	8 ounces

SCOOP TABLE

Scoops are universal in size. The chart below shows the ones I use the most. The scoop number corresponds to the number of scoops in a quart.

Scoop #	Colour	Diameter (inches)	Oz	Tbsp	Cup	mL	Scoops/Cup
20		2 1/8	1 2/3	3 1/5	1/5	47	5
24		2	1 1/3	2 3/4	1/6	39	6
40		1 5/8	2/3	1 2/3	1/10	24	10

TWO CAKE RECIPES, TWO BUTTERCREAMS, A HANDFUL OF FILLINGS & FROSTING RECIPES—EVERYTHING YOU WILL NEED TO CREATE THIRTY-EIGHT CAKES OR CUPCAKES PLUS VARIATIONS.

Over the course of several years, I developed and tested these recipes. They have proven to be trustworthy and delicious.

Understanding the basics of baking is truly the key. But baking the cake is only half the battle.

When it comes to filling the cake, your imagination is the only thing holding you back. Fillings don't just look more professional; they also create different textures and flavours within a single bite of cake.

Keep in mind that the cakes and the fillings will all need to be premade and cooled before you put them together.

The batter for each cake is enough to make two dozen cupcakes; the assembly directions for the cupcakes are included in each recipe.

Once you've got the hang of some of these basic recipes, switch it up. I encourage you to step outside your comfort zone and create new flavour combinations. And please be sure to share your discoveries with me.

Of course, you can still enjoy a plain vanilla or chocolate cake with a vanilla buttercream!

This, my friends, is a game changer, this will change the way you bake . . . this will change the way you see the world!

I used to either grease and flour my pans or take the time to parchment-line them every time I wanted to bake. And gosh, I bake a lot of cakes! Goop truly changed my life. And I'm willing to bet that you already have the ingredients in your cupboard!

What is Goop? It's a homemade cake release. You can buy national brand cake releases, but chances are that you have the three ingredients you need *in* your cupboard. Not to mention the cost savings! Yup . . . three simple ingredients will *change your life*!

GOOP

Vegetable **oil**
All-purpose **flour**
Vegetable **shortening**

1 Use equal parts of each ingredient. I typically use one cup of each. This makes a substantial amount, but you can store it.

2 Put all three ingredients into a mixer and blend until smooth.

3 Store in an airtight container in the cupboard at room temperature. Goop can last a long time if it's stored properly.

GOOP IT—AND THANK ME LATER

Simply take a pastry brush and lightly paint the insides of the pans with the mixture before pouring in your cake batter.

That's it . . . really . . . I promise you. Three ingredients, three steps. Life changed! No more wasted time.

note If you notice there is separation in the mixture after it has been sitting for a while (the oil will sometimes separate out, the way a natural nut butter does), just stir until incorporated.

SIMPLE SYRUP

Simple syrup—sugar syrup, flavour injector, moisture adder, cake saver, whatever you want to call it—is so . . . simple to make. But there are so many amazing benefits to using it.

If you are a drink connoisseur or were ever a mixologist in your life, you are quite familiar with simple syrup. It is a common ingredient in many mixed drinks.

Simple syrup can add another layer of flavour or a little more moisture to the cake. It helps enhance an already great cake and can prolong the cake's shelf life.

I typically make a large batch and pop it in the refrigerator, then I have it on hand when needed. After I've made the basic mix, I flavour it as desired.

Water
Sugar
Vanilla

1   Use equal parts of water and sugar—for example, 1 cup of water and 1 cup of sugar. Heat gently in a saucepan on the stove, stirring occasionally, until sugar is dissolved.

2   Once the sugar is completely dissolved, add a splash of vanilla. The bigger the batch, the bigger the splash! I don't ever measure this, but if I were to guess, I would say about ½ tsp vanilla per cup of syrup.

3   Place in the refrigerator to cool completely. When ready to use, pour into a squeeze bottle with a small nozzle. And you're set!

Vanilla cake is one of the most challenging cakes to get right. Everyone searches for that perfect balance of structure, **crumb**, and moistness . . . for that perfect "cake-mix cake."

This vanilla cake is the perfect addition to anyone's recipe box! And this recipe has been developed and tweaked to allow it to be made ahead of time and refrigerated. This breaks all the rules of baking: once a leavener like baking powder is added, you are supposed to bake right away. I have had no issues with premaking this batter and using it up to three days later. Doing this allows me to prep ahead of time and bake the cake fresh when I need it.

CLASSIC VANILLA CAKE

YIELD TWO TO THREE 8" ROUND CAKES (DEPENDING ON THE ADDITIONS) OR 24 CUPCAKES

1 cup vegetable or canola **oil**

2 cups granulated **sugar**

4 large **eggs**

1 Tbsp **vanilla**

1 cup **milk**

2¼ cups all-purpose **flour**

6 Tbsp **cornstarch**

1 Tbsp **baking powder**

½ tsp **salt**

1   Preheat oven to 350°F.

2   Goop the base and sides of the pan.

3   Combine oil, sugar, and eggs in a mixer on medium low until blended. Add vanilla and milk and mix.

4   In a separate bowl, sift the flour, cornstarch, baking powder, and salt. Add to the sugar and egg mixture and mix.
Do not overmix, as this will result in a dry, tough cake and tunnel-like holes in the baked cake.

For Cakes • Goop cake tin, pour batter in until two-thirds full, bake for 30 to 40 minutes, or until toothpick comes out clean.

note Each recipe will tell you how many pans to goop and split the batter into. Baking time will vary based on the amount of batter in each pan.

For Cupcakes • Line 24 cupcake cups with paper or foil liners. Scoop the batter into each lined cup using your yellow scoop. If you are not using a scoop, then fill each cupcake cup about two-thirds full. Bake for 17 to 19 minutes, or until a toothpick comes out clean.

Crumb means the inside of the cake, how dense or loose the cake is.

The search for the ultimate chocolate cake that isn't dry and crumbly but has a rich chocolate flavour was a tough one. In fact, I never did find one I truly liked. Finally, I came up with this brilliantly moist, rich, dark-chocolate cake.

The key ingredient that really makes this cake is coffee! Adding hot coffee to the batter helps enhance the flavour of the chocolate. It's not enough coffee to make the cake mocha flavoured, just enough to elevate that rich cocoa. Adding the hot liquid also helps dissolve the sugar, making for a smoother, more uniform batter.

CHOCOLATE CAKE

1   Preheat oven to 350°F.

2   Combine oil, sugar, and eggs in a mixer on medium low until blended.

3   Add vanilla, buttermilk, and coffee. Mix on low until blended.

4   In a separate bowl, sift together the flour, cocoa powder, baking soda, baking powder, and salt. Add to the mixer and mix just until blended. *Do not overmix, as this will result in a dry, tough cake and tunnel-like holes in the baked cake.*

YIELD TWO TO THREE 8" ROUND CAKES (DEPENDING ON THE ADDITIONS) OR 24 TO 30 CUPCAKES

1 cup vegetable or canola **oil**

2 cups **sugar**

2 large **eggs**

4 tsp **vanilla**

1 cup **buttermilk**

1 cup **hot coffee**

2½ cups all-purpose **flour**

¾ cup **cocoa powder**

2 tsp **baking soda**

1 tsp **baking powder**

1 tsp **salt**

For Cakes • Goop cake tin, pour batter in until two-thirds full, bake for 30 to 40 minutes, or until toothpick comes out clean.

note Each recipe will tell you how many pans to goop and split the batter into. Baking time will vary based on the amount of batter in each pan.

For Cupcakes • Line 24 to 30 cupcake cups with paper or foil cupcake liners. Scoop batter into each lined cup using your red scoop. If you are not using a scoop, then fill each cupcake cup about half full. Bake for 15 to 17 minutes, or until a toothpick comes out clean.

Don't have buttermilk?

In one-cup measuring cup, put 1 Tbsp cider vinegar and fill to 1 cup with room-temperature milk. Allow to sit for 10 to 15 minutes. Stir and use in place of buttermilk.

Old-school frosting . . . in my neck of the woods that means American Buttercream. This is the traditional frosting that Mama might have made!

This recipe has the perfect sweetness and is very versatile. And if you make it a few days ahead of time, it doesn't require refrigeration! But if you plan to make it a few days in advance or find yourself with leftovers, you can refrigerate or freeze it.

AMERICAN BUTTERCREAM

YIELD ABOUT **8 CUPS**

1 cup unsalted **butter**, softened

1 cup vegetable **shortening**, softened

½ tsp **salt**

2 tsp **vanilla**

2 to 6 Tbsp **heavy cream**, divided

8 cups **icing sugar**, divided

note A stand mixer is strongly recommended for buttercream.

1   Mix the butter and shortening on high for 6 minutes.

2   Scrape the sides of the bowl and add the salt, vanilla, and half of the heavy cream. Mix on low until incorporated and then on high for about 6 minutes or until the mixture has tripled in size. It should be smooth, creamy, and white.

3   Add half of the icing sugar. Mix on low—just until incorporated and smooth.

4   Add the other half of the icing sugar, again mixing just until incorporated and smooth. This will help reduce the number of air bubbles in the final buttercream.

5   Adjust the consistency by pouring in some extra heavy cream.
Add a little at a time and mix on low to avoid extra air.

6   Use immediately or store in an airtight container for future use.

note If you store American Buttercream for longer than a few days, you will need to remove it from the refrigerator or freezer, allow it to warm up, and mix it in the mixer until smooth again.

Avoid splatter To avoid splatter all over the kitchen, place a tea towel over the mixer.

SWISS MERINGUE BUTTERCREAM

Meringue-based buttercreams are a little trickier because you use egg whites to create them. I prefer the Swiss method, so here we have Swiss Meringue Buttercream.

This buttercream is not as sweet as the traditional American Buttercream. Unlike the American version, it does require constant refrigeration once the cake is prepared.

YIELD ABOUT 6 CUPS

6½ oz **egg whites** (approximately 6 large egg whites)

8 oz granulated **sugar**

¼ tsp **salt**

3½ oz vegetable **shortening**

1 lb unsalted **butter**, softened

2 tsp **vanilla**

note A stand mixer is strongly recommended for buttercream.

1   Place the egg whites, sugar, and salt into the bowl of the mixer. Place the bowl over a pot of simmering water and heat gently while whisking continuously to avoid scrambling the eggs. As the egg mixture warms, place your thumb and index finger in and feel the egg mixture for grit—undissolved sugar.

2   Keep whisking until the egg mixture is smooth. Transfer the bowl to a stand mixer with a whisk attachment and turn on medium high.

3   Whip the mixture to stiff peaks and until the meringue comes down to room temperature.

4   Switch to a paddle attachment. Add the shortening and butter a little at a time until well combined.

5   Add the vanilla and beat until smooth.

note The mixture may appear curdled. This is normal; just keep mixing and the buttercream will come together and become smooth and creamy.

CHOCOLATE GANACHE

Sometimes life calls for something a little more decadent . . . a little richer and more indulgent than buttercream. Don't get me wrong, buttercream is great, but ganache . . . ganache is in a league of its own. Sometimes it's a necessity in the cake for stability—like creating a dam that helps keep the filling inside the cake. At other times, you just want to add another layer of depth and richness.

Here are the ratios for the varying types of ganache. These amounts should be measured by weight using a scale. For example, if you use milk chocolate for a firm ganache, then combine 3 pounds of chocolate to 1 pound of heavy cream.

Type of Chocolate	Texture of Ganache	Ratio of Chocolate to Heavy Cream
Semi-Sweet/ Dark Chocolate	Firm	2:1
	Soft	1:1
Milk Chocolate	Firm	3:1
	Soft	2:1
White Chocolate	Firm	4:1
	Soft	3:1

1   Heat the heavy cream gently, stirring occasionally to ensure it doesn't burn. *Be careful that you don't allow the heavy cream to boil, as it will boil over onto the stove, and trust me, that's a mess you don't want to clean up.*

2   Break chocolate into pieces and place it in a heat-proof bowl. Once the heavy cream is hot—*not* boiling—carefully pour it over the chocolate and stir. Let the mixture sit for a few minutes to allow the heavy cream to melt the chocolate, and then stir until smooth. *Use the mixer on low speed, as you don't want to splash hot heavy cream all over yourself.*

3   Allow the mixture to cool. As it cools, it will set and become pipeable or spreadable, depending on your desired use.

note It's important to use a good-quality chocolate for ganache. Try to avoid chocolate chips, as they have additives that keep them from melting properly—they are usually designed to hold their shape during baking.

CREAM CHEESE FROSTING

There is no replacing the delicious tang that cream cheese provides. In the world of desserts—and food in general—the constant struggle is to find balance within the dish.

With cakes that have many components, it's not hard to take it a little too far and end up with something overly sweet. This is easily rectified by choosing to use a cream cheese frosting rather than a traditional one. The tangy zip it provides can help cut through the sweetness of the rest of the dessert.

YIELD ABOUT 7 CUPS

¼ cup unsalted **butter**, softened

8 oz **cream cheese**, softened

Pinch of **salt**

2 tsp **vanilla**

1 to 3 Tbsp **heavy cream**

8 cups **icing sugar**, divided

1   Mix the butter and cream cheese on high for 4 minutes.

2   Scrape the sides of the bowl and add the salt, vanilla, and 1 tablespoon of the heavy cream.

3   Mix on low until incorporated and then on high for 5 minutes or until about triple in size. It should be smooth, creamy, and white.

4   Add half of the icing sugar. Mix on low—just until incorporated and smooth.

5   Add the other half of the icing sugar, again mixing just until incorporated and smooth. This will help reduce the air bubbles in the final frosting.

Adjust the consistency of the frosting by adding more heavy cream. Add a little at a time and mix on low, again to avoid extra air.

note Use immediately or refrigerate in an airtight container for future use. If this frosting is stored, you will need to remove it from the refrigerator, allow it to warm up, and mix it in the mixer until smooth again.

Fruit curds are typically made with citrus fruit: lemons, limes, oranges.

Thinking about the entire composition of the cake is key: get the right balance of sweet, savoury, and sour to ensure balance.

When you make a curd for cake, it is usually best to keep it on the sour side, so that it pairs well with sweeter ingredients.

Fruit curds are probably my favourite, especially lemon. Traditionally, a curd is made up of citrus juice, eggs, sugar, and a thickening agent. It is cooked until thick and allowed to cool to a smooth creamy spread.

Feel free to experiment with any of the citrus fruits—limes or oranges make great curds as well!

LEMON CURD

YIELD 1 TO 1½ CUPS

5 large **egg yolks**

1 large **egg**

1½ tsp **cornstarch**

The zest and freshly squeezed juice of 2 to 3 **lemons** (⅓ cup). For ease, zest before you squeeze!

⅓ cup to ½ cup granulated **sugar**

3 Tbsp unsalted **butter**, chopped

1   Combine the egg yolks, whole egg, cornstarch, zest, and juice in a saucepan.

note Save the egg whites; they can be frozen and used for Swiss Meringue Buttercream.

2   Add the sugar (amount based on the desired sweetness) and cook over medium heat, whisking continuously until thick (about 5 minutes).

3   Remove from heat and fold the butter into mixture.

4   Strain into a bowl using a mesh strainer or sieve.

5   Cover with plastic wrap. Be sure that the plastic is touching the top of the curd to avoid a skin forming.

6   Place in the refrigerator to cool completely before using.

Squeeze with Ease

Heat the citrus gently before squeezing it: place the whole fruit in the microwave for 20 to 30 seconds. This will make the process easier, and you will maximize the amount of juice.

Pastry cream, or custard, is a thickened milk-and-egg-based filling similar to pudding, but with more eggs.

My pastry cream won over the judges on *Spring Baking Championship*: Duff Goldman asked for the recipe, Lorraine Pascale said that she's "stealing the idea," and Nancy Fuller said it was like nothing she'd ever tasted before, and "brilliant."

Here I give you my brown-sugar cream-cheese pastry cream. This is amazing as a filling in a cake, but it can also be used in a custard tart topped with your favourite fresh berries.

PASTRY CREAM

YIELD ABOUT 2 CUPS

5 large **egg yolks**

3 Tbsp **cornstarch**

6 Tbsp **brown sugar**, divided

1¼ cups **whole milk**, divided

4 oz **cream cheese** (½ block), softened

2 Tbsp unsalted **butter**, softened

1 tsp **vanilla**

1   Whisk the yolks, cornstarch, and 3 tablespoons of the brown sugar together in a medium bowl.

   note *Save the egg whites; they can be frozen and used for Swiss Meringue Buttercream.*

2   Add ¼ cup of the milk and whisk until smooth. Set aside.

3   Separately, combine the remainder of the milk and brown sugar in a medium saucepan. Bring just to a simmer over medium heat. Do *not* allow this to boil or it will spill over. Remove from heat.

4   Add roughly one-quarter cup of the hot-milk mixture to the egg-yolk mixture while whisking continuously. Add another quarter cup of hot mixture and whisk.

5   Pour into the saucepan with the rest of the hot-milk mixture and stir.

6   Bring to a boil, stirring constantly. Cook for one to two minutes, until thickened.

7   Remove from heat, add the cream cheese, butter, and vanilla, and whisk until smooth.

8   Strain into a bowl using a mesh strainer or sieve, and cover the surface with plastic wrap to prevent a skin from forming. Refrigerate until completely cooled.

Don't want the caramel undertones from the brown sugar?
Simply replace it with white—or, to deepen the flavour, use dark.

....

The process of mixing small amounts of hot liquids into cold gradually is called *Tempering* *and is done to help reduce the risk of scrambling the eggs.*

CARAMEL SAUCE

Caramel is a classic, and next to chocolate, it's one of everyone's favourite sweet treats. It comes in so many forms: hard candy, soft and chewy, or a sauce that you can pour on just about anything!

I like to use a nice thick caramel sauce to mix into my buttercream for a delicious flavour.

Or, if you're a fan of the sweet and salty, add a few extra pinches of your favourite sea salt to give you that oh-so-perfect salted caramel.

I also love using this as an added sauce between layers of cake, dripping down the sides, or drizzled over the top of a cupcake!

YIELD ABOUT 1 CUP

⅔ cup packed **brown sugar**

5 Tbsp **heavy cream**

¼ cup unsalted **butter**

Pinch **salt** (up to 1 tsp for salted caramel)

1 tsp **vanilla**

1   Mix the brown sugar, heavy cream, butter, and salt in a saucepan over medium-low heat.

2   Whisk gently for five to seven minutes until the mixture gets thick and smooth.

Be careful when adding the vanilla; the caramel will spit and bubble up quickly.

3   Add the vanilla, stir another minute. Allow to cool completely before using.

FRUIT FILLING

Fruit fillings add a wonderful pop of flavour to a cake. However, they can't be too sweet or too runny, or they won't work for structural purposes. Fruit fillings should be on the tarter side to balance the sweetness of the cakes and frostings.

This base recipe can be used with almost any fruit.

YIELD ABOUT 1 CUP

Fruit, fresh or frozen, approximately 2½ cups

Zest and juice of ½ **lemon**

¼ tsp **salt**

¼ cup granulated **sugar**

....

Cornstarch slurry (1 Tbsp **cornstarch** + 2 Tbsp **cold water**)

Mix ingredients in a bowl, and it's ready to use.

1   Combine the fruit, lemon zest and juice, salt, and sugar, and cook on medium heat until the fruit is completely broken down and juices are slightly reduced or thickened.

> *note* *You can make the cornstarch slurry while the fruit mixture is cooking.*

2   Add the slurry to the boiling fruit mixture and cook for two to three minutes until thick and bubbly. Remove from heat and cool completely in the refrigerator.

CANDY BAR

COLLECTION

CANDY BARS ARE PROBABLY SOME OF THE FIRST MEMORIES MOST OF US HAVE OF SWEET TREATS.

The pesky things are a staple in every corner store, right there by the checkout at every supermarket!

Whether they create good memories or bad, candy bars aren't going anywhere. There are hundreds of flavours, but we all have our absolute favourite. These bar inspirations are among some of my family's favourites.

COOKIES 'N' CREAM CAKE • PAGE 57

TURTLE CAKE
PAGE 63

ALMOND JOY CAKE • PAGE 48

COFFEE CRISP CAKE • PAGE 54

TERRY'S CHOCOLATE
ORANGE CAKE
• PAGE 61

CHERRY BLOSSOM CAKE   PAGE 51

An Almond Joy, not to be confused with a Mounds bar, is a chocolate-covered coconut bar topped with almonds. Chewy coconut centre, crunchy almond, and silky chocolate. How much more delicious does it need to get? The incredible texture of the coconut centre is one of the main reasons I chose this candy bar to recreate in cake.

ALMOND JOY CAKE

1 batch of **Chocolate Cake batter** plus 1¼ cups of shredded **coconut**, divided evenly into two 8" gooped pans and baked

½ batch of **Swiss Meringue Buttercream** plus ¾ tsp to 1 tsp almond extract, to taste

2 lbs of firm **Dark-Chocolate Ganache**

1 batch of **Coconut Filling**, divided

½ cup **Toasted Slivered Almonds** (page 50), plus additional ½ cup for decoration

Macaroons (page 50) and **coconut** for decoration

COCONUT FILLING

1 can of **sweetened condensed milk**

2½ cups shredded **coconut**

½ tsp **salt**

1 tsp **vanilla**

Mix all ingredients in a bowl, and it's ready to use.

Cake Assembly

1   Level and torte the cakes, giving you four layers.

2   Spread a small amount of buttercream onto the cake plate so the first layer of cake sticks to it.

3   Layer the cake as follows:

cake

half of the buttercream

cake

ganache, piped into a dam around the edge (See Damming and Filling, page 15)

half of the coconut filling, in the centre

cake

half of the buttercream

cake

4   Place in the refrigerator for 15 to 20 minutes before crumb-coating. This will help stabilize the cake and set the buttercream so the layers don't slide apart while finishing.

5   Crumb-coat the cake with a thin layer of ganache and place back in the refrigerator for 10 to 15 minutes.

6   Remove from the refrigerator, and add the final layer of ganache. Create a horizontal line pattern on the finished coat of ganache.

Frost the cake with a smooth ganache finish, but don't be too picky, as you are not leaving it like this.

→ While slowly spinning the turntable, hold the angled spatula against the frosting at a slight angle—allowing the tip to press into the ganache.

→ As you rotate the cake, move the spatula up slightly until you reach the top.

→ Use the same method on the top of the cake, moving from the outside to the centre.

7   Place most of the almonds at the bottom edge of the cake. Place baked macaroons in a pile in the centre of the cake. Place the rest of the almonds and coconut on the top edge, and you are done!

Cupcake Assembly

1   Core each cupcake using an apple corer.

2   Place the buttercream in a piping bag with no tip, and fill each cupcake.

3   Pipe a nest of buttercream around the edge of each cupcake with a 1M tip.

4   Fill the nest with a spoonful of coconut filling.

5   Drizzle with a little ganache.

6   Sprinkle with toasted almonds.

TOASTED SLIVERED ALMONDS
*Place a single layer of **almonds** on a lined sheet pan. Bake at 350°F for 8 to 10 minutes, stirring halfway through. Allow to cool.*

MACAROONS
*Take the second half-batch of **coconut filling**. With a purple scoop, place scoops of the filling onto a baking sheet lined with parchment paper, and bake at 350°F until golden brown, about 15 to 20 minutes.*

For as long as I can remember, this has been my mom's go-to chocolate treat. She would bite the side off and slurp the candy filling from inside and then pop out the cherry. My father-in-law especially enjoyed these! He was always sure to get a box of Queen Annes (the close cousin to the Blossom) just for himself under the Christmas tree each year. Being the kind of man he was, he never could keep them from his kids! They would always ask, and Dad was sure to tell them "Yes b'y, go ahead."

CHERRY BLOSSOM CAKE

1 batch of **Chocolate Cake batter** plus 1¼ cups of shredded **coconut**, divided evenly into three 8" gooped pans and baked

Cherry brandy or other liqueur (optional)

1 batch of **Swiss Meringue Buttercream**, divided:

To half the batch, add 1 Tbsp maraschino cherry juice, ½ cup finely chopped maraschino cherries, and 1 tsp almond extract.

To a quarter of the batch, add 3 Tbsp of smooth peanut butter.

To a quarter of the batch, add 2 tsp coconut flavouring.

2½ lb of firm semi-sweet **Chocolate Ganache** (reserve 1½ cups)

To the remainder, add ½ cup chopped peanuts and ⅓ cup fine toasted coconut.

For cupcakes, make 1 lb of chocolate ganache and add ¼ cup of chopped peanuts and 3 Tbsp of fine toasted coconut.

1 batch of **Cherry Cream Filling** (page 52)

Maraschino cherries with stems for decoration

Cake Assembly

1   Level and torte the cakes, giving you six layers.

note Optional: Brush each cake layer with cherry brandy or other cherry liqueur.

2   Spread a small amount of buttercream onto the cake plate so the first layer of cake sticks to it.

3   Layer the cake as follows:

cake

half of the cherry buttercream

cake

all of the peanut-butter buttercream

cake

plain chocolate ganache, piped into a dam around the edge (See Damming and Filling, page 15)

cherry cream filling, in the centre

cake

all of the coconut buttercream

cake

half of the cherry buttercream

cake

CHERRY CREAM FILLING

*You will need 2½ cups **icing sugar**, 4 Tbsp **maraschino cherry juice**, 2 Tbsp **corn syrup**, 1½ Tbsp unsalted **butter**, melted, 2 tsp **almond extract**, ½ tsp **vanilla**, and ½ tsp **salt**.*

Mix all the ingredients until well combined. You will end up with a smooth cream that should ribbon when you pour.

4   Place in the refrigerator for 20 to 30 minutes before crumb coating. This will help stabilize the cake and set the buttercream so the layers don't slide apart while finishing.

5   Crumb-coat the cake with a thin layer of the plain chocolate ganache and place back in the refrigerator for 10 to 15 minutes.

6   Remove from the refrigerator and ice the cake using the chocolate-peanut ganache. Create a smooth finish to mimic the look of an actual Cherry Blossom. The pieces in the ganache will keep it from being completely smooth.

7   With a purple scoop, place dollops of leftover ganache around the outer edge, and add a cherry to each dollop.

Don't have a scoop? Just roll balls of ganache in your hands!

Cupcake Assembly

1   Core each cupcake using an apple corer.

2   Place the cherry cream filling into a piping bag with no tip, and fill each cupcake.

3   Place each of the buttercreams and the ganache in its own separate piping bag, each with a 1A tip.

4   Pipe a circle of each of the four toppings in the following order, getting gradually smaller each time.

chocolate ganache

peanut-butter buttercream

coconut buttercream

cherry buttercream

5   Place a cherry on top. Use the ones with stems for effect.

1½ batches of **Classic Vanilla Cake batter** plus the following additions, mixture divided evenly into three 8" gooped pans and baked

6 tsp of **instant coffee** dissolved in 2 tsp **hot water**

12 **vanilla wafer cookies**, roughly chopped

....

For cake, make 1 batch of **American Buttercream**, *divided:*

To half of the batch, add 1½ Tbsp **instant coffee** *dissolved in 1½ tsp* **hot water**.

To half of the batch, add ¾ cup **cocoa powder** *and 2 to 3 Tbsp* **heavy cream**.

For cupcakes, make 1 batch of **American Buttercream**, *divided:*

To three-quarters of the batch, add 1 Tbsp **instant coffee** *dissolved in 1 tsp* **hot water**.

To the remaining quarter, add ½ cup **cocoa powder** *and 1 to 2 Tbsp* **heavy cream**.

....

½ cup **Simple Syrup** plus 2 tsp of **instant coffee** dissolved in ½ tsp **hot water**

4 to 6 **vanilla wafer cookies**, roughly chopped

1 oz of **semi-sweet chocolate**, melted, for decoration

Additional **wafer cookies** for decoration

This candy bar was always my favourite. The layers of crispy wafers, the light coffee flavour, and the delicate chocolate covering make for the perfect bite.

For the cake, I had to be sure I incorporated that wafer aspect. What better way than with sandwich wafer cookies? I could sit and eat these by the hundreds; maybe that's why the coffee crisp bar is my favourite!

COFFEE CRISP CAKE

Cake Assembly

1   Level the cakes.

2   Spread a small amount of buttercream onto the cake plate so the first layer of cake sticks to it.

3   Layer the cake as follows:

cake—soaked in syrup

half of the coffee buttercream

chunks of wafer cookie, sprinkled

cake—soaked in syrup

half of the coffee buttercream

chunks of wafer cookie, sprinkled

cake—soaked in syrup

4   Place in the refrigerator for 15 to 20 minutes before crumb-coating. This will help stabilize the cake and set the buttercream so the layers don't slide apart while finishing.

5   Crumb-coat the cake with a thin layer of the chocolate buttercream and place back in the refrigerator for 10 to 15 minutes.

6   Remove from the refrigerator and add a final layer of chocolate buttercream. Frost with a rough or rustic style.

7   Cut the extra vanilla wafer cookies at random lengths and place them in a half-moon pattern. This gives the cake a little more height and movement.

8   Place the melted chocolate in a piping bag. Cut a small hole in the end, and with even pressure drizzle the chocolate over the wafer cookies.

Cupcake Assembly

1   Brush the top of each cupcake with syrup, then core the cupcakes using an apple corer.

2   Place the chocolate buttercream in a piping bag with no tip, and fill each cupcake.

3   Put the coffee buttercream into a piping bag with a 1A tip, and pipe a large swirl.

4   Insert a chunk of vanilla wafer.

5   Drizzle with melted chocolate.

I would say this one is more enjoyable in its cookie form than the bar form, but either will fill a good craving. This cake flavour is one of my most popular. Who can resist huge chunks of Oreo *in* their cake? It's the best of both worlds! The beauty of baking the cookies into the cake batter itself is that the cookies become soft, just like the cake, but you can still pick out the distinctive flavour of the actual cookie.

COOKIES 'N' CREAM CAKE

1 batch of **Classic Vanilla Cake batter** plus 10 to 12 roughly crushed **Oreo cookies**, divided evenly into three 8" gooped pans and baked

1 batch of **American Buttercream**, divided:

*To one-half of the batch (for filling), add 3 to 4 roughly crushed **Oreo cookies** (some chunks and some crumb).*

*To the other half (for frosting), add 4 **Oreo cookies** crushed into a fine crumb.*

*For cupcakes, make a full batch of **American Buttercream** and add 8 finely crushed **Oreos**.*

½ cup **Simple Syrup** (not required for cupcakes)

1 lb of soft semi-sweet **Chocolate Ganache**

Cookies 'n' cream treats, **Oreo cookies**, reserved **buttercream**, and **sprinkles** for decoration

2 to 3 dozen **Mini Oreos** (for cupcakes only)

Cake Assembly

1   Level the cakes.

2   Spread a small amount of buttercream onto the cake plate so the first layer of cake sticks to it.

3   Layer the cake as follows:

cake—soaked in syrup

⅓ cup ganache, thinly spread

half of the filling buttercream

cake—soaked in syrup

⅓ cup ganache, thinly spread

half of the filling buttercream

cake—soaked in syrup

4   Place in the refrigerator for 15 to 20 minutes before crumb-coating. This will help stabilize the cake and set the buttercream so the layers don't slide apart while finishing.

5   Crumb-coat the cake with the frosting buttercream and place back in the refrigerator for 10 to 15 minutes.

6   Remove from the refrigerator and add the final layer of the filling buttercream. Frost with a smooth finish.

7 Set in the freezer for 15 to 20 minutes. The cake should be cold to help set the chocolate ganache when added.

8 Warm the ganache gently until you can pour it.

*You **do not** want a hot ganache. If it is too warm, it will simply fall to the bottom of the cake and not give you any variations. Feel the chocolate—you need it to be about room temperature.*

9 Pour ganache into a squeeze bottle with a nozzle top and create drips along the side of the cake.

10 Squeeze a large pool of ganache on top centre of the cake. Use an offset spatula to evenly spread it, being careful not to push it over the edge, as it will ruin the perfect drips.

11 Place an array of Oreo treats in a crescent moon pattern. Pipe dollops of the reserved frosting among the other treats.

Cupcake Assembly

1 Put the buttercream in a piping bag with a 1A piping tip, and pipe a classic swirl on top of the cupcake.

2 Place the cooled ganache in a squeeze bottle with nozzle and squeeze the ganache over the top of the cupcake.

3 Insert a Mini Oreo into the ganache.

For a good swirl on top of the cupcake, it's important to keep constant pressure on the bag as your hand moves in circles.

You used to wait all year to get your hands on these chocolatey treats. This cake is a dream. The combination of vanilla cake and orange chocolate ganache transports you right back to that happy place.

I use vanilla cake because chocolate cake might compete for the top spot in flavour central. Vanilla is a great vehicle to let the rest of the flavours shine.

TERRY'S-CHOCOLATE-ORANGE CAKE

1 batch of **Classic Vanilla Cake batter**, divided evenly into two 8" gooped pans and baked

1 batch of **American Buttercream** plus 1 to 1½ Tbsp of **orange extract** and 3 to 4 drops of **orange gel food colour** for a light orange colour

½ cup of **Simple Syrup** plus zest of half an **orange** and 1 tsp **orange extract** or shot of orange liqueur

1 lb of semi-firm semi-sweet **Chocolate Ganache** (ratio 1½:1) plus 2 to 3 tsp of **orange extract**, to taste

Chocolate Sails (page 62) for decoration

Cake Assembly

1   Level and torte the cakes, giving you four layers.

2   Spread a small amount of buttercream onto the cake plate so the first layer of cake sticks to it.

3   Layer the cake as follows:

cake—soaked in syrup

one-third of the ganache

cake—soaked in syrup

one-quarter of the buttercream

cake—soaked in syrup

one-third of the ganache

cake—soaked in syrup

4   Place in the refrigerator for 15 to 20 minutes before crumb-coating. This will help stabilize the cake and set the buttercream so the layers don't slide apart while finishing.

5   Crumb-coat the cake with a thin layer of buttercream and place back in the refrigerator for 10 to 15 minutes.

6   Remove from the refrigerator and add the final layer of buttercream. Frost with a smooth finish, leaving a lip at the top to contain the ganache. Do not bother to frost the top of the cake, as you will cover it in ganache.

7   Create a diagonal line striation pattern by dragging the tip of an angled spatula through the buttercream from bottom to top. Continue until you complete the entire side of the cake.

8   Gently heat the remainder of the ganache until runny, and pour it on the top of the cake until the ganache smoothly covers the entire top of the cake. The lip of buttercream stops it from dripping over.

Be careful not to overheat the ganache or you will "break" it, which means the ingredients will separate.

9   Place the chocolate sails into the top of the cake.

CHOCOLATE SAILS
*Melt 6 oz of **semi-sweet chocolate** until smooth.*

Spread the chocolate thinly onto a silicone baking mat.

Using clothes pins, pinch the edges of the mat into random shapes and set on a sheet pan until the chocolate is firm.

Cupcake Assembly

1   Brush the top of each cupcake with the syrup using a pastry brush. This is a lot less messy than using a squeeze bottle.

2   Ensure the ganache has set enough to hold its shape, and place it in a piping bag with a 1A piping tip.

3   Place the buttercream in another piping bag fitted with a 1M piping tip.

4   First, pipe a round disk of ganache onto each cupcake, then pipe a small swirl of the buttercream directly on top.

5   Decorate by inserting two to three of the homemade chocolate sails. *Or* you could grab a couple of chocolate oranges and stick a wedge on top.

Another true holiday classic in my house growing up, and another one of my mom's favourites.

The pecan is the best part . . . The velvety chocolate smothering the luscious caramel and the light crunch of the pecan are a match made in heaven. You can't go wrong turning this classic treat into a cake and filling it full of caramel and pecan goodness.

1 batch of **Chocolate Cake batter**, divided evenly into two 8" gooped pans and baked

1 batch of **Swiss Meringue Buttercream** plus 10½ oz of melted semi-sweet chocolate

½ cup of **Simple Syrup** plus 3 Tbsp **Caramel Sauce** (syrup not required for cupcakes)

2 cups of toasted **pecan halves**

3 batches (about 3 cups) of homemade or store-bought **Caramel Sauce**, 1 cup reserved

¾ cup *very* roughly chopped **pecans** for decoration (not required for cupcakes)

TURTLE CAKE

Cake Assembly

1   Level and torte the cakes, giving you four layers.

2   Spread a small amount of buttercream onto the cake plate so the first layer of cake sticks to it.

3   Layer the cake as follows:

cake—soaked in syrup

thin layer of buttercream, so the caramel won't seep into the cake

buttercream, piped into a dam around the edge (See Damming and Filling, page 15)

1 cup of pecan halves

1 cup of the caramel sauce

cake—soaked in syrup

1 cup of buttercream

cake—soaked in syrup

buttercream, thinly spread

buttercream dam, piped around the edge

1 cup of pecan halves

1 cup of the caramel sauce

cake—soaked in syrup

4   Place in the fridge for 15 to 20 minutes before crumb-coating. This will help stabilize the cake and set the buttercream so the layers don't slide apart while finishing.

5   Crumb-coat the cake with a thin layer of buttercream and place back in the refrigerator for 10 to 15 minutes.

6   Remove from the refrigerator and add the final layer of buttercream. Frost with a smooth finish.

7   Set in the freezer for 15 to 20 minutes. The cake should be cold enough so that it helps set the caramel sauce when added.

8   Warm the caramel sauce gently until you can pour it.

9   Pour the caramel sauce into a squeeze bottle with a nozzle top and create drips along the side of the cake.

10 Squeeze a large pool of caramel sauce on the top of the cake. Use an offset spatula to evenly spread it, being careful not to push it over the edge, as it will ruin the perfect drips.

11 Finally, place a ring or wreath of roughly chopped pecans on top of the cake.

Cupcake Assembly

1   Core each cupcake using an apple corer.

2   Reserve one pecan half per cupcake; roughly chop remaining pecans.

3   Fill each cupcake centre about ½ full with chopped pecans, leaving room to add delicious caramel.

4   Place the caramel, cooled but still liquid, into a squeeze bottle with nozzle top, and fill each cupcake with caramel sauce.

5   Place the buttercream in a piping bag fitted with the 1M piping tip and pipe a classic swirl on top of the cupcake.

6   Drizzle caramel sauce over the top of the cupcake.

7   Insert a pecan half.

This will satisfy any ooey-gooey caramel craving you've ever had!

CLASSIC DESSERTS REIMAGINED

WE ALL HAVE A FAVOURITE DESSERT, BAKED GOOD, OR SWEET TREAT THAT BRINGS US COMFORT.

Simply saying *cake* isn't specific enough—it is very broad.

Usually, comfort foods are not cake; they are foods like warm cinnamon rolls, maybe Nanaimo bars, or fire-roasted S'mores.

In this section, I take some favourite classic treats and reinvent them as dessert cakes.

TIRAMISU CAKE • PAGE 87

NANAIMO-BAR CAKE • PAGE 84

CAMPFIRE S'MORE CAKE • PAGE 73

BOSTON-CREAM-PIE CAKE • PAGE 70

GERMAN CHOCOLATE CAKE • PAGE 80

CINNAMON-ROLL CAKE • PAGE 76

It's called pie, but is really a cake . . . No matter what you call it, it's delicious! The light, fluffy vanilla cake paired with the rich, smooth, velvety pastry cream is made complete when drowned in a bold semi-sweet chocolate ganache.

Although it's a classic already—the amazing pastry cream gives it a twist.

BOSTON-CREAM-PIE CAKE

1 batch of **Classic Vanilla Cake batter**, divided evenly into two 8" gooped pans and baked

½ lb soft semi-sweet **Chocolate Ganache**

½ cup of **Simple Syrup** (not required for cupcakes)

2 batches of **Pastry Cream** (reserve one cup for your puffs)

1 batch of **Mini Cream Puffs** for decoration (homemade or store-bought)

MINI CREAM PUFFS
Makes 24-30 puffs

½ cup **water**

¼ cup unsalted **butter**

¼ tsp **salt**

½ cup all-purpose **flour**

1 cup of **Pastry Cream** (see above)

2 **eggs**

To Make Mini Cream Puffs

1 Preheat the oven to 375°F.

2 In a saucepan, bring the water, butter, and salt to a boil.

3 Add the flour and cook, stirring continuously until the mixture starts to create a film on the bottom of the pan.

4 Transfer the mixture to a mixer bowl with paddle attachment.

5 Mix on medium low for 5 minutes. Then add the eggs one at a time until mixture becomes a smooth paste. Continue mixing for an additional 2 minutes.

6 Transfer the cream-puff dough (*pâte à choux*) to a piping bag with a 1A piping tip.

7 On a parchment-lined baking sheet, pipe small dollops of dough (roughly the size of a tablespoon).

note Leave three inches of space around the dollops, as the dough will triple in size.

8 Place the baking sheet on the middle rack and bake for 15 to 20 minutes. The puffs should be golden and hollow.

9 Turn off the oven, prop the door open with a wooden spoon, and leave the puffs to cool.

10 Once puffs are completely cooled, poke a hole in the bottom of each one, using a small piping tip, such as a #8, or a knife.

11 Place the pastry cream in a piping bag with no tip and cut the end. Fill each puff with pastry cream.

Grab yourself a nice
big cup of joe and a rather
large slice of cake,
and indulge yourself!

12   Your cream puffs are now ready for any recipe or on their own. If using for this recipe, dip the tops in your prepared ganache and refrigerate.

Cake Assembly

1   Level and torte the cakes, giving you four layers.

2   Spread a small amount of ganache onto the cake plate so the first layer of cake sticks to it.

3   Layer the cake as follows:

cake—soaked in syrup

1 cup pastry cream

cake—soaked in syrup

1 cup pastry cream

cake—soaked in syrup

1 cup pastry cream

cake—soaked in syrup

note Be careful not to push the pastry cream over the edge of the cake, as this will be a naked cake.

4   Place in the refrigerator for 25 to 30 minutes to set and chill before adding the ganache. This will help stabilize the cake and set the pastry cream so the layers don't slide apart while finishing.

5   Remove from the refrigerator and pour ganache on top of the cake. With an offset spatula, gently push the ganache to the edge of the cake; allow for a little ganache to fall over the sides. Don't coat all the sides: just have a few drips coming down.

Cupcake Assembly

1   Core each cupcake using an apple corer.

2   Place the pastry cream in a piping bag with no tip, and fill each cupcake.

3   Put the ganache in a piping bag with a 1A tip, and pipe a flat disk on top of each cupcake.

4   While the ganache is still a little sticky, place a cream puff on the top of each cupcake.

We don't get out on family camping trips as much as I would love to. Between work, life, and the kids' schedules, it's just not in the cards as much as we wish. That doesn't stop us from having backyard fires or even beach fires, and of course S'mores are a must-have.

CAMPFIRE S'MORE CAKE

2 batches of **Graham Crumb Crust** (page 74)

For cupcakes, 1 batch of Graham Crumb Crust

- -

1 batch of **Chocolate Cake batter**

For cake, divide the batter evenly into two 8" gooped pans with Graham Crumb Crust at the bottom of each pan, and bake.

For cupcakes, press 1 Tbsp of Graham Crumb Crust into the bottom of each lined cupcake cup, pour the batter in, and bake.

- -

1 batch of **American Buttercream**, divided:

One-half with Toasted Mini Marshmallows (page 75) *mixed in*

One-half with 1 cup of **dark cocoa** *and 2 to 3 Tbsp of* **milk** *or heavy cream mixed in*

- -

½ cup of **Simple Syrup** (not required for cupcakes)

One 7½ oz bottle of **marshmallow fluff**, warmed for spreading

Additional **mini marshmallows** and **graham crumbs** for decoration

Cake Assembly

1   Level and torte the cakes, giving you four layers. Two will have graham crumb bases, two will be plain.

2   Spread a small amount of buttercream onto the cake plate so the first layer of cake sticks to it.

3   Layer the cake as follows:

cake with graham crumb base—soaked in syrup

half of the marshmallow buttercream

cake—soaked in syrup

chocolate buttercream, piped into a dam around the edge (See Damming and Filling, page 15)

marshmallow fluff, filled in the centre

cake with graham crumb base—soaked in syrup

half of the marshmallow buttercream

cake—soaked in syrup

4   Place in the refrigerator for 15 to 20 minutes to set before crumb-coating. This will help stabilize the cake and set the buttercream so the layers don't slide apart while finishing.

5   Crumb-coat the cake with a thin layer of chocolate buttercream and place back in the refrigerator for 10 to 15 minutes.

6   Remove from refrigerator and add the final layer of chocolate buttercream. Frost with a smooth finish.

7   Then try to create a finish on the sides that resembles tree bark.

→   Before the frosting stiffens, take an angled spatula and stick it vertically onto the buttercream and pull it away while moving upward towards the top of the cake. Repeat this all the way around the cake.

8   Create a wreath of mini marshmallows around the cake. Fill with graham crumbs.

9   Lightly toast some of the marshmallows with a torch. Be careful not to melt the buttercream.

GRAHAM CRUMB CRUST

*You will need 1½ cups of **graham crumbs**, ¼ cup unsalted **butter**, melted, 2 Tbsp granulated **sugar**, and a pinch of **salt**.*

Place all the ingredients in a bowl and mix.

TOASTED MINI MARSHMALLOWS

*You will need 1½ cups of **mini marsh-mallows**. Place a single layer of marsh-mallows on a lined baking sheet. Place in the oven on broil. **Do not** walk away, as they will burn quickly. Take them just past the golden stage.*

Cupcake Assembly

1   Core each cupcake using an apple corer.

2   Put marshmallow fluff in a piping bag with no tip, and fill each cupcake.

3   Put marshmallow buttercream in a piping bag fitted with a 1A piping tip, and pipe a disk of buttercream on each cupcake.

4   Put chocolate buttercream in a piping bag fitted with a 6B piping tip, and pipe a small swirl on top of the marshmallow buttercream.

5   Top with a sprinkle of graham crumbs.

6   Add a few mini marshmallows. Lightly toast some of the marsh-mallows with a torch. Be careful not to melt the buttercream.

Cozy up to the fire,
grab yourself a slice of
cake, and dream of
warm summer nights.

One of the best parts about making fresh cinnamon rolls: the warm smell of cinnamon flowing through the kitchen.

Take those sweet-smelling bundles of cinnamon joy out of the oven, and smother them in a cream cheese frosting while still warm.

This cake will bring you all the joys of a fresh-baked cinnamon roll while still satisfying your cake cravings too.

CINNAMON-ROLL CAKE

1 batch of **Classic Vanilla Cake batter** and 1 batch of **Cinnamon Butter** (page 77), layered together in three 8" gooped pans and baked

To do this layering, put the Cinnamon Butter in a squeeze bottle and squeeze it out in spirals.

½ cup of **Simple Syrup** (not required for cupcakes)

1½ batches of **Cream Cheese Frosting**

1 batch of **Cinnamon Spread** (page 77)

1 batch of **Mini Cinnamon Rolls** for decoration (store-bought two-bite rolls will also work)

MINI CINNAMON ROLLS

1 cup all-purpose **flour**

2 Tbsp granulated **sugar**

½ tsp **salt**

1½ Tbsp unsalted **butter**, cold

6 Tbsp cold **milk**

2 Tbsp unsalted **butter**, softened

½ cup **Cinnamon Mix** (page 77) plus some for decoration

To Make Mini Cinnamon Rolls

1. In a bowl, combine the flour, sugar, and salt.

2. Cut in the cold butter.

3. Add the cold milk and mix until just combined.

4. Roll dough out on a lightly floured surface to about ¼" thick.

5. Spread the softened butter on the dough and sprinkle with the cinnamon mix.

6. Roll tightly.

7. Slice cinnamon rolls roughly ½" wide each and lay flat on a gooped baking sheet.

8. Bake at 350°F for 8 to 12 minutes until a light golden brown.

9. Remove from oven and allow to cool completely.

Cake Assembly

1. Level and torte the cakes, giving you four layers.

2. Spread a small amount of cream cheese frosting onto the cake plate so the first layer of cake sticks to it.

A little extra decoration

Thin out some of the frosting with milk or heavy cream until runny, place in a squeeze bottle, and drizzle over the top.

CINNAMON MIX

You will need 1 cup granulated **sugar**, *1 cup* **brown sugar**, *2½ Tbsp* **cinnamon**, *and 5 tsp* **cocoa**.

Place all ingredients in a bowl and whisk until well combined.

CINNAMON BUTTER

You will need ⅓ cup unsalted **butter**, *melted, and ¾ cup* **Cinnamon Mix**.

Pour the butter into a squeeze bottle, add the Cinnamon Mix, and shake.

CINNAMON SPREAD

You will need ½ cup **cream cheese**, *softened, 1½ Tbsp unsalted* **butter**, *softened, and ½ cup* **Cinnamon Mix**.

Place all ingredients into a bowl and mix until well combined.

3   Layer the cake as follows:

cake—soaked in syrup

half of the cinnamon spread, spread thinly

about ¾ cup cream cheese frosting

cake—soaked in syrup

half of the cinnamon spread, spread thinly

about ¾ cup cream cheese frosting

cake—soaked in syrup

4   Place in the fridge for 15 to 20 minutes to set up before crumb-coating. This will help stabilize the cake and set the frosting so the layers don't slide apart while finishing.

5   Crumb-coat the cake with a thin layer of cream cheese frosting and place back in the refrigerator for 10 to 15 minutes.

6   Remove from the refrigerator and add the final layer of frosting. Finish the cake in a rosette pattern, leaving the top with a relatively smooth surface.

7   Evenly place the cinnamon rolls around the perimeter of the cake and dust with a sprinkle of cinnamon mix.

Cupcake Assembly

1   Spread a thin layer of cinnamon spread on top of each cupcake.

2   Place the cream cheese frosting in a piping bag with a 1M piping tip, and pipe a rosette on top of each cupcake.

3   Add a mini cinnamon roll to finish it off.

4   Sprinkle with a little cinnamon mix.

Most believe that this cake comes from Germany. Truth be told, the cake dates back only about sixty to seventy years and originates in Texas.

It's called German chocolate because of the chocolate that was once used to make the cake itself—again not German, but named after the man who created it.

A German chocolate cake consists of layers of moist chocolate cake filled with a coconut and pecan caramel custard and finished off with a silky-smooth chocolate buttercream. Things don't get much more decadent than this.

GERMAN CHOCOLATE CAKE

1 batch of **Chocolate Cake batter**, divided evenly into two 8" gooped pans and baked

½ batch of **American Buttercream** plus 1 cup of **cocoa** and 2 to 3 Tbsp of **milk** or heavy cream

½ cup of **Simple Syrup** (not required for cupcakes)

1 lb semi-firm **Dark-Chocolate Ganache** (ratio 1½:1), cooled and set

1 batch of **Coconut Caramel Pecan Custard**

Candied Pecans, for decoration (store-bought or see page 81)

COCONUT CARAMEL PECAN CUSTARD

1 cup **evaporated milk** (canned milk)

1 cup **brown sugar**

½ cup unsalted **butter**, melted

1 Tbsp **cornstarch**

1 tsp **vanilla**

¼ tsp **salt**

2 large **egg yolks**

1 large whole **egg**

1¼ cups shredded **coconut**

1¼ cups chopped **pecans**

To Make Coconut Caramel Pecan Custard

1   Place milk, brown sugar, butter, cornstarch, vanilla, salt, and eggs (yolks and whole) in a medium saucepan over medium heat and gently whisk. Continue to cook the mixture until it gently starts to bubble. The mixture will thicken and coat the back of a wooden spoon.

note It is important to whisk mixtures with eggs continuously while heating, so as not to scramble the eggs.

2   Remove from heat and strain the mixture through a mesh sieve into a heat-proof bowl.

3   Mix in coconut and pecans.

4   Cover with plastic wrap, ensuring the wrap touches the surface of the custard so a skin does not develop. Allow it to cool completely in the refrigerator.

Cake Assembly

1   Level and torte the cakes, giving you four layers.

2   Spread a small amount of buttercream onto the cake plate so the first layer of cake sticks to it.

CANDIED PECANS

*You will need ½ cup **brown sugar**, 1 Tbsp **corn syrup**, ¼ tsp **salt**, ¼ tsp **cinnamon**, 2 Tbsp **water**, 1 tsp **vanilla**, and 1 cup **pecan halves**.*

Place brown sugar, corn syrup, salt, cinnamon, water, and vanilla in a saucepan over medium heat. Allow to boil until sugar mixture becomes viscous and bubbles start slowly popping (3 to 5 minutes once boiling starts).

Remove from heat, add the pecan halves, and mix thoroughly. Spread evenly onto parchment paper or a silicone baking mat, and allow to cool completely.

3   Layer the cake as follows:

cake—soaked in syrup

half the ganache

cake—soaked in syrup

ganache, piped into a dam around the edge
(See Damming and Filling, page 15)

half the custard, filling in the centre

cake—soaked in syrup

remainder of ganache

cake—soaked in syrup

4   Place in the refrigerator for 15 to 20 minutes to set before crumb-coating. This will help stabilize the cake and set the ganache so the layers don't slide apart while finishing.

5   Crumb-coat the cake with a thin layer of buttercream and place back in the refrigerator for 10 to 15 minutes.

6   Remove from the refrigerator and add another layer of buttercream. Create a horizontal line finish.

7   Create a wreath of piped buttercream using a piping bag with a 1M tip. Fill the wreath with the remainder of the custard. Place candied pecans around the top of the cake and drizzle the entire cake in ganache.

Cupcake Assembly

1   Core each cupcake using an apple corer.

2   Place the ganache in a piping bag with no tip, and fill each cupcake.

3   Place the buttercream in a piping bag fitted with a 1M tip, and pipe a ring around the edge of each cupcake.

4   With a purple scoop, drop the custard into the centre of the ring.

5   Drizzle with ganache and place a candied pecan on top.

This classic Canadian dessert bar originated in British Columbia. Of course, I had to pay homage to this incredible delight: a chocolate cake laden with toasted walnuts and shredded coconut, layered with a creamy custard buttercream, and smothered in a rich chocolate ganache!

NANAIMO-BAR CAKE

1 batch of **Chocolate Cake batter** plus the following additions, divided evenly into three 8" gooped pans and baked

1 cup shredded **coconut**

¾ cup toasted chopped **walnuts**

- - - - - - - - - - - - - - - - - -

1 batch of **American Buttercream** plus ½ cup of **custard powder** and 8 to 10 Tbsp of **milk**, or until spreadable

½ cup of **Simple Syrup** (not required for cupcakes)

½ lb soft semi-sweet **Chocolate Ganache**

1 batch of **Nanaimo Bar Base**

NANAIMO BAR BASE

½ cup unsalted **butter**, melted

¼ cup granulated **sugar**

⅓ cup **cocoa**

1 large **egg**

2 tsp **vanilla**

½ tsp **salt**

1 cup **graham crumbs**

1½ cups shredded **coconut**

½ cup toasted chopped **walnuts**

To Make the Nanaimo Bar Base

1   Combine butter, sugar, and cocoa in top of a double boiler.

2   Add the egg and stir to cook and thicken, about 1 to 2 minutes.

note Keep the heat low enough that you don't scramble the egg.

3   Remove from heat and add vanilla and salt. Stir in the graham crumbs, coconut, and walnuts.

4   Press firmly into a parchment-lined 8" x 8" pan.

5   Refrigerate until cooled and firm.

6   Remove from the pan, and chop into various sizes and shapes as desired.

Cake Assembly

1   Level the cakes.

2   Spread a small amount of buttercream onto the cake plate so the first layer of cake sticks to it.

3   Layer the cake as follows:

cake—soaked in syrup

1 cup of buttercream

cake—soaked in syrup

1 cup of buttercream

cake—soaked in syrup

4 Place in the refrigerator for 15 to 20 minutes to chill before adding the crumb coat. This will help stabilize the cake and set the buttercream so the layers don't slide apart while finishing.

5 Crumb-coat the cake with a thin layer of buttercream and place back in the refrigerator for 10 to 15 minutes.

6 Remove from the refrigerator and add the final layer of buttercream. Frost with a smooth buttercream to allow for nice drips when ganache is added.

7 Place in the freezer for 15 to 20 minutes. The cake should be cold enough so that it helps to set the chocolate when added.

8 Warm the ganache gently until you can pour it.

9 Pour ganache into a squeeze bottle with a nozzle top and create drips along the side of the cake.

10 Squeeze a large pool of ganache onto the top of the cake. Use an offset spatula to evenly spread it, being careful not to push it over the edge, as it will ruin the perfect drips.

11 Place chunks of the Nanaimo bar base on the top and randomly along the sides of the cake.

Cupcake Assembly

1 Put the buttercream in a piping bag with a 1A tip, and pipe a buttercream blob on top of each cupcake.

2 Place the room-temperature ganache in a squeeze bottle and squeeze over the top of each cupcake. You want it to drip down the sides of the frosting but not fully cover it.

3 Place a couple of chunks of Nanaimo bar base on the top of each cupcake.

The classic tiramisu transports us all the way to Italy, where the sweet ladyfingers are soaked in a coffee mixture, layered with an egg-based mascarpone cream, and dusted with cocoa.

This version of a tiramisu is a classic vanilla cake soaked in a coffee syrup, layered with mascarpone meringue buttercream, and beautifully adorned with chocolate-dipped ladyfingers. Don't panic, I won't make you bake your own ladyfingers!

TIRAMISU CAKE

1 batch of **Classic Vanilla Cake batter**, divided evenly into three 8" gooped pans and baked

1 batch of **Swiss Meringue Buttercream** plus 1¼ cups mascarpone cheese

¾ cup of **Simple Syrup** plus 1½ Tbsp **instant coffee** dissolved in 1 tsp **hot water**

3 Tbsp **dark rum**, amaretto, or Kahlúa (optional)

20 to 24 store-bought **ladyfingers**

semi-sweet chocolate for dipping (optional)

Cocoa for dusting

Satin ribbon

Cake Assembly

1 Level the cakes.

2 Spread a small amount of buttercream onto the cake plate so the first layer of cake sticks to it

3 Layer the cake as follows:

cake—soaked in a generous amount of syrup
....
1 cup of buttercream
....
cake—soaked in a generous amount of syrup
....
1 cup of buttercream
....
cake—soaked in a generous amount of syrup

4 Place in the refrigerator for 15 to 20 minutes to set before crumb-coating. This will help stabilize the cake and set the buttercream so the layers don't slide apart while finishing.

5 Crumb-coat the cake with a thin layer of buttercream and place back in the refrigerator for 10 to 15 minutes.

6 Remove from the refrigerator and add the final layer of buttercream. Frost with a smooth finish, but there's no need to be perfect, as you will be adding a lot of decoration!

Dip it! Dip the ladyfingers in melted semi-sweet chocolate for additional flavour. Allow to set on parchment until firm.

7   Place the ladyfingers side by side all the way around the cake.

note *If dipping them in chocolate, dip them first, and face the chocolate side in.*

8   Place the cocoa in a mesh sieve and lightly dust the top of the cake.

9   Tie a satin ribbon around the cake, for aesthetics and to keep those ladyfingers from falling of.

Cupcake Assembly

1   Generously brush each cupcake with simple syrup.

2   Place the buttercream in a piping bag fitted with a 6B piping tip, and pipe a semi-swirl on top.

3   Dust with cocoa.

4   Insert half a ladyfinger in the centre.

This cake is truly the perfect gift to unwrap at the end of a delicious meal.

CLASSIC PAIRINGS

SO MANY CLASSIC FLAVOUR COMBINATIONS BRING BACK MEMORIES AND LEAVE US DAYDREAMING OF BEING RIGHT THERE.

Some classic flavours and foods out there are just meant to sing together in perfect harmony of both balance and taste.

The perfect pairs: peanut butter and chocolate, salt and caramel, peanut butter and jam, strawberries and chocolate, bread and butter, chicken and waffles, potatoes and gravy . . . (Writing a cakebook makes you hungry!)

SALTED-CARAMEL CAKE
• PAGE 110

MILK-AND-COOKIES
CAKE • PAGE 101

STRAWBERRY,
WHITE-CHOCOLATE
AND PINK-CHAMPAGNE
CAKE • PAGE 113

DARK-CHOCOLATE
AND HONEY CAKE
• PAGE 98

CHOCOLATE, PEANUT-
BUTTER AND PRETZEL
CAKE • PAGE 94

PEANUT-BUTTER AND
JAM CAKE • PAGE 106

Need I say more? Truly this speaks for itself.

To ensure we truly get that chocolate and peanut-butter experience, this is a marble cake, but not the traditional marble of course: a rich peanut-butter cake marbled with the moist chocolate cake.

CHOCOLATE, PEANUT-BUTTER AND PRETZEL CAKE

½ batch of **Chocolate Cake batter**

½ batch of **Classic Vanilla Cake batter** plus ½ cup smooth **peanut butter**

Divide the 2 batters evenly into three 8" gooped pans by alternating— adding a little bit of one batter and then of the other. When all the batter is in the pans, swirl a butter knife through it to create a marbled effect. Bake.

note When using the knife, be careful not to drag it across the bottom of the pan and scratch it.

1½ batch of **American Buttercream** plus 2½ cups of **dark cocoa** and enough **heavy cream** to make it smooth and spreadable

½ cup **Simple Syrup** plus ½ cup of smooth **peanut butter** (syrup not required for cupcakes)

1 batch of **Peanut-Butter-Crunch Filling** (page 95)

½ cup of smooth **peanut butter** for decoration

Chocolate Pretzel Bark (page 95) for decoration

Semi-Dipped Pretzels (page 96) or store-bought chocolate-dipped pretzels for decoration

Cake Assembly

1   Level and torte the cakes, giving you six layers.

2   Spread a small amount of buttercream onto the cake plate so the first layer of cake sticks to it.

3   Layer the cake as follows:

cake—soaked in syrup

1 cup of buttercream

cake—soaked in syrup

half of the peanut-butter-crunch filling

cake—soaked in syrup

1 cup of buttercream

cake—soaked in syrup

half of the peanut-butter-crunch filling

cake—soaked in syrup

1 cup of buttercream

cake—soaked in syrup

4   Place in the refrigerator for 15 to 20 minutes to set before crumb-coating. This will help stabilize the cake and set the buttercream so the layers don't slide apart while finishing.

PEANUT-BUTTER-CRUNCH FILLING

*You will need 1 cup smooth **peanut butter**, 3 Tbsp unsalted **butter**, softened, 1 cup **icing sugar**, ½ tsp **vanilla**, ¼ tsp **salt**, 1 cup **Rice Krispies**, and 1 cup coarsely crushed store-bought **Chocolate-Covered Pretzels**.*

Cream the peanut butter, butter, icing sugar, vanilla, and salt in a mixer on medium high until nice and smooth. Scrape the side of the bowl and add Rice Krispies and pretzels. Mix on low until combined.

CHOCOLATE PRETZEL BARK

*You will need ½ lb **semi-sweet chocolate**, melted, 1 bag (300 g) **peanut-butter chips**, divided, and **pretzels**, plain or chocolate-dipped, for decoration.*

Melt half the bag of peanut-butter chips in a separate bowl from the chocolate and reserve some for decoration.

Spread the melted semi-sweet chocolate on a parchment-lined baking sheet, drizzle the melted peanut-butter chips over the chocolate, and swirl with a toothpick.

While the chocolate is still wet, sprinkle it with some crushed pretzels and extra peanut-butter chips.

Allow to set fully before breaking into random shaped pieces.

SEMI-DIPPED PRETZELS

You will need 12 to 18 large **salted pretzels***, 1 cup* **semi-sweet chocolate***, melted, and ½ bag* **peanut-butter chips***, melted.*

Dip half a pretzel in the semi-sweet chocolate and set it on a parchment-lined baking sheet. Repeat with remaining pretzels.

Drizzle the half-dipped pretzels with melted peanut-butter chips. Allow the chocolate to cool completely.

note You can buy chocolate-dipped pretzels if you wish, and simply use them as they are or drizzle them with melted peanut-butter chips.

5   Crumb-coat the cake with a thin layer of buttercream and place back in the refrigerator for 10 to 15 minutes.

6   Remove from the refrigerator and add the final layer of buttercream. Frost with a smooth finish.

7   Set in the freezer for 15 to 20 minutes. The cake should be cold enough so that it helps to set the peanut-butter drip.

8   Warm the peanut butter gently until you can pour it.

9   Pour the peanut butter into a squeeze bottle with a nozzle top and create drips along the side of the cake.

10 Squeeze a large pool of peanut butter on the top centre of the cake. Use an offset spatula to evenly spread it, being careful not to push it over the edge, as it will ruin the perfect drips.

11 Place varying size pieces of bark and pretzels in the centre of the cake. Arrange some on the sides if you wish.

Cupcake Assembly

1   Core each cupcake using an apple corer.

2   Put peanut-butter-crunch filling into a piping bag with no tip, and fill each cupcake.

3   Put the buttercream in a piping bag fitted with a 1M tip, and pipe a classic swirl onto the top of each cupcake.

4   Insert a chunk of bark and a pretzel.

5   Drizzle with warmed peanut butter.

Peanut butter and honey are great, but seriously . . . This will change your point of view on dark chocolate. Dark chocolate tends to be bitter and earthy and not palatable by many, and that's where honey steps up to change your mind. The natural sweetness pairs beautifully and harmoniously.

DARK-CHOCOLATE AND HONEY CAKE

1 batch of **Chocolate Cake batter**, divided evenly into two 8" gooped pans and baked

¼ batch of **Swiss Meringue Buttercream** plus 3 to 4 Tbsp of **honey**, to taste

½ cup of **Simple Syrup** plus 2 Tbsp **honey** (syrup not required for cupcakes)

2 lbs **Dark-Chocolate and Honey Ganache** (page 99), cooled and set

....

1 batch **Caramel Sauce** plus ¼ cup **honey**

Add the honey while the sauce is boiling.

....

Honeycomb Candy for decoration

HONEYCOMB CANDY

1¼ cup granulated **sugar**

½ cup **honey**

Pinch of **salt**

1 Tbsp of **baking soda**, sifted (Yes really, sift it!)

1 tsp **vanilla**

To Make the Honeycomb Candy

1   Goop a baking sheet and keep it nearby.

2   In a large pot, boil the sugar, honey, and salt.

3   Stir it with a silicone spatula for even caramelization until the mixture turns an autumn brown (295°F on a candy thermometer), about 3 minutes.

4   Remove from heat and add the baking soda and vanilla.

   Be careful! The baking soda is going to react and bubble up quite a bit.

5   Stir gently until baking soda is fully dissolved, but not so much that you deflate the mixture.

6   Pour onto the baking sheet and set for about 15 minutes.

7   Break into random-sized pieces.

Cake Assembly

1   Level and torte the cakes, giving you four layers.

2   Spread a small amount of buttercream onto the cake plate so the first layer of cake sticks to it.

3   Layer the cake as follows:

   cake—soaked in syrup

   ¾ cup of ganache

   cake—soaked in syrup

   1 cup buttercream

   cake—soaked in syrup

   ¾ cup of ganache

   cake—soaked in syrup

DARK-CHOCOLATE AND HONEY GANACHE

Cakes: Ratio of 3:1 with half the heavy cream replaced by **honey**

Cupcakes: Ratio of 2:1 with half the heavy cream replaced by **honey**

4   Place in the refrigerator for 15 to 20 minutes to set before crumb-coating. This will help stabilize the cake and set the ganache and the buttercream so the layers don't slide apart while finishing.

5   Crumb-coat the cake with half the remainder of the ganache and place back in the refrigerator for 10 to 15 minutes.

6   Remove from the refrigerator and add the final layer of ganache. Frost with a smooth finish.

7   Set in the freezer for 15 to 20 minutes. The cake should be cold enough so that it helps to set the caramel sauce when added.

8   Pour the caramel sauce in the centre of the cake and, using an offset spatula, evenly spread it carefully out to the edge of the cake, gently pushing some over the edges from time to time. This will create a very organic drip.

9   Place varying size pieces of honeycomb candy in a cluster on the top of the cake. Arrange some on the sides if you wish.

Cupcake Assembly

1   Core each cupcake using an apple corer.

2   Place the ganache in a piping bag with no tip, and fill each cupcake, reserving ½ cup of ganache for step 6.

3   Put the buttercream in a piping bag fitted with a 1A tip, and pipe a blob onto the top of each cupcake.

4   Spoon cooled caramel sauce over the top of each cupcake.

5   Insert a nice chunk of honeycomb candy.

6   Drizzle with warmed ganache.

1 batch of **Classic Vanilla Cake batter** plus 1½ Tbsp ground **cinnamon**, divided evenly into two 8" gooped pans and baked

*For cupcakes, place baked 2" round **Melt-in-Your-Mouth Shortbread Cookies** (page 102) in the bottom of lined cupcake pans before scooping in the cake batter.*

1 batch of **American Buttercream**, divided:

*To two-thirds of the batch, add ¼ cup **milk powder** dissolved in 3 Tbsp **warm water**.*

*To the other third, add 6 to 8 roughly crushed **Oreo cookies**.*

½ cup **Simple Syrup** plus 2 Tbsp **milk powder**, dissolved in 2 Tbsp **hot water** (syrup not required for cupcakes)

1 batch of **Eggless Cookie Mixture** (some baked for decoration, remainder left unbaked)

2 batches of **Melt-in-Your-Mouth Shortbread Cookies** (page 102) baked as two 6.5" round disks and a few small ones for decoration

1 batch **Cake-Mix Snickerdoodles** (page 102)

Various cookies—whole, halves, and crumbles, for decoration, including mini cookies if you're making cupcakes

EGGLESS COOKIE MIXTURE

½ cup unsalted **butter**, softened

¼ cup granulated **sugar**

½ cup packed **brown sugar**

1½ cups cooked **flour**

Bake the flour on a parchment-lined baking sheet at 285°F for 8 minutes. Allow to cool before use.

1 tsp **baking soda**

2 tsp **vanilla**

¼ cup **milk**

2 Tbsp vegetable **oil**

1 cup **mini chocolate chips**

Although it's not truly a flavour classic, you can't have cookies without a nice cold glass of milk.

It's so satisfying to hold the cookies in the milk until they're nice and soft, then drink the milk at the end . . . slightly flavoured by the cookies and a few surprise crumbs at the bottom that we have no trouble consuming as well!

This cake features my most sought-after cookie recipe, as seen on Food Network's *Spring Baking Championship*: Melt-in-Your-Mouth Shortbread Cookies.

MILK-AND-COOKIES CAKE

To Make the Eggless Cookie Mixture

1   Preheat oven to 350°F.

2   Combine the butter, sugars, baked flour, baking soda, vanilla, milk, and oil in a mixer bowl, and mix on medium speed until a smooth dough forms.

3   Scrape the sides of the bowl and mix in the mini chocolate chips on low speed. This dough will be used as a filling, but we will also bake 12 cookies for decoration.

4   Scoop 12 tablespoon-sized balls onto a baking sheet and gently flatten. Bake for 10 to 12 minutes, turning the pan halfway through. Once golden, remove and cool completely.

5   Do not bake the rest of the dough. Press it into a disk about the size of the cake.

note If the mixture is too dry, add more milk to soften it.

MELT-IN-YOUR-MOUTH SHORTBREAD COOKIES

¾ cup unsalted **butter**, softened

½ cup **icing sugar**

1 tsp **vanilla**

1 cup + 2 Tbsp all-purpose **flour**

½ cup **cornstarch**

¼ tsp **salt**

CAKE-MIX SNICKERDOODLES

1 package of **vanilla/ white cake-mix**

½ cup unsalted **butter**, melted

1 large **egg**

½ tsp **vanilla**

2 Tbsp **brown sugar**

1 tsp ground **cinnamon**

½ tsp **cocoa**

Pinch of **salt**

To Make Melt-in-Your-Mouth Shortbread Cookies

1. Preheat oven to 350°F.

2. Cream together the butter and icing sugar.

3. Add the vanilla and mix.

4. Sift together the flour, cornstarch, and salt. Add to the butter mixture and combine.

5. Wrap the dough in plastic and chill in the refrigerator for 15 to 20 minutes.

6. Roll the dough to ¼" thick on a lightly floured surface to make two 6½" round disks and a few small ones for decoration. Or, if making cupcakes, make 24 2" cookies and 24 mini cookies, each ½" to 1" round.

7. Bake for 10 to 12 minutes, turning the pan halfway through, remove from the oven, and allow to cool completely.

To Make Cake-Mix Snickerdoodles

1. Preheat oven to 350°F.

2. Mix the cake mix, butter, egg, and vanilla until dough forms.

3. Put the dough in the refrigerator to firm up slightly for 10 to 15 minutes.

4. Roll the dough into small balls, varying sizes for decoration.

5. Mix the brown sugar, cinnamon, cocoa, and salt. Toss each ball of cookie dough in the cinnamon mixture.

6. Place on a gooped cookie sheet about 2 to 3 inches apart—cookies will spread during baking.

7. Bake for 10 to 12 minutes, turning the pan halfway through.

8. Remove from the oven, and allow to cool completely before serving.

9. Store leftovers in an airtight container

Cake Assembly

1 Level and torte the cakes, giving you four layers.

2 Spread a small amount of buttercream onto the cake plate so the first layer of cake sticks to it.

3 Layer the cake as follows:

cake—soaked in syrup
....
⅔ cup of Oreo buttercream
....
shortbread disk
....
⅔ cup of Oreo buttercream
....
cake—soaked in syrup
....
⅔ cup of milk-flavoured buttercream
....
disk of eggless cookie mixture
....
⅔ cup of milk-flavoured buttercream
....
cake—soaked in syrup
....
⅔ cup of Oreo buttercream
....
shortbread disk
....
⅔ cup of Oreo buttercream
....
cake—soaked in syrup

4 Place in the refrigerator for 15 to 20 minutes to set before crumb-coating. This will help stabilize the cake and set the buttercream so the layers don't slide apart while finishing.

5 Crumb-coat the cake with a thin layer of the milk buttercream and place back in the refrigerator for 10 to 15 minutes.

6 Remove from the refrigerator and add the final layer of milk butter-cream. Frost with a rough-style buttercream.

→ Put some milk buttercream on top of the cake and smooth it out.

→ Use a large spatula, smear dollops of the buttercream onto the sides of cake. Repeat this pattern until the cake is completely covered.

7 Arrange cookies all over the top, varying sizes and pieces, chunks, and crumbs. Cookie heaven!

Cupcake Assembly

1   Core each cupcake using an apple corer.

2   Put the Oreo buttercream into a piping bag with no tip, and fill each cupcake.

3   Place a disk of unbaked eggless cookie mixture on top of the cupcake.

4   Put the milk buttercream into a piping bag with a 1A tip, and pipe a blob on top of the eggless cookie disk.

5   Finish the cupcakes with various mini cookies.

It's a tale as old as time . . . I mean, who doesn't like a good PB&J sandwich? I know I ate my body weight in them through my elementary and high school years.

PEANUT-BUTTER AND JAM CAKE

1 batch of **Classic Vanilla Cake** batter plus 1 cup of smooth **peanut butter**, divided evenly into three 8" gooped pans and baked

....

1½ batch of **Swiss Meringue Buttercream**, divided:

To two-thirds of the batch, add ¼ cup of the raspberry Fruit Filling (see below) or use your favourite store-bought jam.

To one-third, add ¼ cup of smooth peanut butter.

....

½ cup **Simple Syrup** (not required for cupcakes)

2 batches of **Fruit Filling** (raspberry) or use your favourite store-bought jam

1 batch of **Pastry Cream**, ¾ cup of smooth **peanut butter** substituted for the cream cheese

Fresh **raspberries** for decoration

Peanut-Butter Cookies for decoration

PEANUT-BUTTER COOKIES

1¼ cups all-purpose **flour**

½ tsp **baking powder**

½ tsp **baking soda**

¼ tsp **salt**

½ cup unsalted **butter**, softened

½ cup granulated **sugar**

½ cup **brown sugar**

½ cup smooth **peanut butter**

1 large **egg**

1 tsp **vanilla**

To Make the Peanut-Butter Cookies

1   Preheat oven to 325°F.

2   Sift the flour, baking powder, baking soda, and salt together in a bowl.

3   In a stand mixer, cream the butter and sugars on medium high until light and fluffy.

4   Add the peanut butter and mix on medium for 45 to 60 seconds.

5   Add the egg and vanilla and mix on low until incorporated.

6   Add the flour mixture and mix on low until dough forms.

7   Chill the dough for 25 to 30 minutes.

8   Remove the dough from the refrigerator and form balls about the size of half a tablespoon. Place them on a parchment-lined baking sheet about two inches apart. Press gently with a fork in two directions to get a cross-hatch pattern on top.

9   Bake for 12 to 15 minutes until golden, turning once halfway through.

Mix it up

In this case, I have used raspberries and raspberry jam, but you could substitute strawberries and strawberry jam or any other fruit that you prefer.

A cake fit for anyone. Break out the picnic basket and enjoy every last mouthful!

Cake Assembly

1 Level and torte the cakes, giving you six layers.

2 Spread a small amount of buttercream onto the cake plate so the first layer of cake sticks to it. Set aside some of both buttercreams for decoration.

3 Layer the cake as follows:

cake—soaked in syrup

raspberry buttercream, piped into a dam around the edge (See Damming and Filling, page 15)

half of the remaining raspberry filling, in the centre

cake—soaked in syrup

peanut-butter buttercream, piped into a dam around the edge

half of the pastry cream, filled in the centre

cake—soaked in syrup

1 cup of raspberry buttercream

cake—soaked in syrup

peanut-butter buttercream, piped into a dam around the edge

half of the pastry cream, filled in the centre

cake—soaked in syrup

raspberry buttercream, piped into a dam around the edge

remaining raspberry filling, filled in the centre

cake—soaked in syrup

4 Place in the refrigerator for 15 to 20 minutes to set before crumb-coating. This will help stabilize the cake and set the buttercream so the layers don't slide apart while finishing.

5 Crumb-coat the cake with either of the buttercreams and place back in the refrigerator for 10 to 15 minutes.

6   Remove from the refrigerator and add final layer of buttercream.
    Frost using a striped buttercream finish.

> →   Place the two types of buttercream in separate piping bags with
>   1A piping tips.

> →   Pipe a strip of one buttercream at the base of the cake, switch to
>   the other buttercream, and pipe another strip.

> →   Repeat this process until you reach the top of the cake and then
>   continue alternating circles of buttercreams on the top as well,
>   going into the centre.

> *note* *Match the outermost buttercream on the top with the last one you
> put on the side. This will make blending them together easier.*

10 Smooth cake as you would any other.

11 Arrange fresh raspberries alternating with peanut-butter cookies
    around the top of the cake.

Cupcake Assembly

1   Core each cupcake with an apple corer.

2   Put the pastry cream and the raspberry filling in separate tipless
    piping bags.

3   Fill the cupcakes halfway with pastry cream, then top them with
    raspberry filling.

4   Place each buttercream in its own bag with no tip. Drop both bags
    down into a third one with a 1A tip. Pipe a swirl on top.

5   Finish with a cookie and a fresh raspberry.

There are those in this world who love their sweets. Then there are those who love their salt. This cake is for those who love them together!

This rich and moist chocolate cake is filled with a delicious homemade caramel buttercream and topped with well . . . more caramel! But the true star here is the salt; get yourself a great-quality sea salt.

1 batch of **Chocolate Cake batter**, divided evenly into three 8" gooped pans and baked

½ batch of **Swiss Meringue Buttercream** plus ¾ cup of **Caramel Sauce**

½ cup of **Simple Syrup** plus 2 Tbsp of **Caramel Sauce** (syrup not required for cupcakes)

2 batches of **Caramel Sauce** plus 1 tsp of **sea salt** in each batch

note ¾ cup is used for the Swiss Meringue Buttercream and 2 Tbsp in the Simple Syrup. The rest is used for drizzling in step 3 and spreading on top in step 7.

Sea salt

SALTED-CARAMEL CAKE

Cake Assembly

1 Level and torte the cakes, giving you four layers.

2 Spread a small amount of buttercream onto the cake plate so the first layer of cake sticks to it. Set aside some buttercream for steps 5 and 6.

3 Layer the cake as follows:

cake—soaked in syrup

1 cup of buttercream

caramel sauce, drizzled

sea salt, sprinkled

cake—soaked in syrup

1 cup of buttercream

caramel sauce, drizzled

sea salt, sprinkled

cake—soaked in syrup

4 Place in the refrigerator for 15 to 20 minutes to set before crumb-coating. This will help stabilize the cake and set the buttercream so the layers don't slide apart while finishing.

5 Crumb-coat the cake with buttercream. This cake is a semi-naked cake; it's nice and simple. Now just frost the top.

6 Place the remaining buttercream in a piping bag with a 1A piping tip and pipe two rows of buttercream dollops in a wreath shape.

note Make sure that the two rows are offset so they make a completely secure dam for the caramel sauce you will be adding next.

7 Fill with the rest of the caramel sauce and sprinkle with a little extra sea salt.

Cupcake Assembly

1 Core each cupcake using an apple corer.

2 Place the cooled caramel sauce into a squeeze bottle with a nozzle top and fill each cupcake. Reserve some sauce for drizzling.

3 Place buttercream in a piping bag with a 1A top and pipe a swirl of buttercream on top of the cupcake.

4 Drizzle with a little more caramel sauce and sprinkle with sea salt.

There's only one thing I can think of that can make champagne and chocolate better than they already are!

Strawberries.

STRAWBERRY, WHITE-CHOCOLATE AND PINK-CHAMPAGNE CAKE

1 batch of **Classic Vanilla Cake batter**, your favourite pink champagne substituted for the milk, plus 1 to 2 drops of **pink food colour gel**, divided evenly into three 8" gooped pans and baked

½ batch of **American Buttercream** plus 6 oz melted **white chocolate**

½ cup of **Simple Syrup** plus 2 Tbsp **champagne** and ½ tsp **strawberry emulsion** (syrup not required for cupcakes)

1 lb **strawberries**, roughly chopped (about pea size)

2 lbs **Strawberry, White-Chocolate and Champagne Ganache** (page 115), cooled and set (for the frosting)

White-chocolate chips or **white-chocolate shavings** for decoration

8 to 10 **Chocolate-Dipped Strawberries** (page 114), or one per cupcake

Cake Assembly

1   Level the cakes.

2   Spread a small amount of buttercream onto the cake plate so the first layer of cake sticks to it.

3   Layer the cake as follows:

cake—soaked in syrup

half the buttercream

half the chopped strawberries

cake—soaked in syrup

half the buttercream

half the chopped strawberries

cake—soaked in syrup

Can't get pink champagne? Any pink sparkling wine will do!

4 Place in the refrigerator for 15 to 20 minutes to set before crumb-coating. This will help stabilize the cake and set the buttercream so the layers don't slide apart while finishing.

5 Crumb-coat the cake with a thin layer of ganache and place back in the refrigerator for 10 to 15 minutes.

6 Remove from the refrigerator and add the final layer of ganache. Before finishing cake, place ½ cup of ganache in a piping bag with a #22 tip.

7 Frost with a smooth finish and a simple rosette pattern.

→ Place some ganache in a piping bag fitted with a #22 tip. Adorn the cake with rosettes and stars that cascade down the front of the cake.

8 Randomly place some white-chocolate chips. Place some chocolate-dipped strawberries where you see fit.

CHOCOLATE-DIPPED STRAWBERRIES

*Melt **white chocolate** and dip clean, dry **strawberries** in the chocolate. Allow to set.*

Drizzle with another colour of chocolate if you wish.

This cake is fit for any celebration, but for romance . . . this is the winner.

Cupcake Assembly

1 Core each cupcake using an apple corer.

2 Fill half the hole with the chopped strawberries.

3 Place the buttercream in a piping bag with no tip, and finish filling each cupcake.

4 Put the ganache in a piping bag with the #22 tip, and pipe a small rosette in the centre. Pipe additional rosettes similar in size to the first one all the way around the top of the cupcake.

5 While the ganache is sticky, place chocolate-dipped strawberries on the top.

STRAWBERRY, WHITE-CHOCOLATE AND CHAMPAGNE GANACHE

*Make the ganache with a ratio of 4:1, but substitute **champagne** for the heavy cream and add 2 tsp **strawberry emulsion** (e.g., LorAnn's emulsions). If you find this too strong, replace only some of the heavy cream.*

HOLIDAYS & CELE-BRATIONS

THIS SECTION FOCUSES ON BOTH FLAVOUR AND AESTHETIC.

The cakes have flavour profiles fitting for each occasion and are then beautifully decorated to suit.

Become the host with the most and wow your party guests with these spectacular cakes.

DEATH-BY-CHOCOLATE CAKE
• PAGE 120

CHRISTMAS TREE
CAKE • PAGE 142

CANADA DAY OR INDEPENDENCE DAY CAKE • PAGE 132

GUINNESS AND BAILEYS
CAKE • PAGE 124

BURROWING BUNNY CAKE
• PAGE 128

WITCHES' BREW CAKE
• PAGE 138

Valentine's Day, the busiest day of the year for chocolatiers and florists!

This cake can be customized to include your favourite chocolates or those of your loved one, because remember—it's for them, not you!

Rich chocolate cake with a layer of brownie thrown in there for extra decadence. The cake is meant to be tall and over the top. You are trying to impress that special someone, right?

VALENTINE'S DAY:

DEATH-BY-CHOCOLATE CAKE

1 batch of **Chocolate Cake batter**, divided evenly into two 8" gooped pans and baked

1½ batches of **American Buttercream** plus 3 cups of **dark cocoa** and ¼ to ½ cup **milk** or heavy cream added a little at a time until it is creamy and spreadable

½ cup **Simple Syrup** plus 3 to 4 Tbsp of **chocolate liqueur** (optional) (syrup not required for cupcakes)

1½ batches of **Brownies** baked in a 9" x 13" pan, cooled, and cut into an 8" circle, with remainder as chunks for decoration

For cupcakes, 1 batch of Brownies, baked in an 8" x 8" pan and cut using the apple corer used to core cupcakes

½ lb soft semi-sweet **Chocolate Ganache**

Chocolates, milk and dark for contrast, for decoration

BROWNIES
½ cup unsalted **butter**

1 cup **sugar**

2 large **eggs**

1 tsp **vanilla**

½ cup all-purpose **flour**

⅓ cup **cocoa**

¼ tsp **baking powder**

¼ tsp **salt**

To Make the Brownies

1   Preheat the oven to 350°F.

2   Goop a 9" x 13" pan on the two longer sides and place parchment paper (approximately 9" x 16") running the length of the pan and up the two shorter sides.

3   Cream the butter and sugar together on medium high.

4   Add the eggs one at a time and mix on medium until combined.

5   Add the vanilla and mix until incorporated.

6   In a separate bowl, sift together the flour, cocoa, baking powder, and salt.

7   Add the flour mixture to the butter/egg mixture and mix *just* until combined. Do not overmix, or the brownie will be tough and dry.

8   Pour into the prepared pan, bake for 25 to 30 minutes, remove from the oven, and allow to cool completely.

Cake Assembly

1   Level and torte the cakes, giving you four layers.

2   Spread a small amount of buttercream onto the cake plate so the first layer of cake sticks to it.

3   Layer the cake as follows:

cake—soaked in syrup

1 cup of buttercream

cake—soaked in syrup

1 cup of buttercream

brownie layer

1 cup of buttercream

cake—soaked in syrup

1 cup of buttercream

cake—soaked in syrup

4   Place in the refrigerator for 15 to 20 minutes to set before crumb-coating. This will help stabilize the cake and set the buttercream so the layers don't slide apart while finishing.

5   Crumb-coat the cake with a thin layer of buttercream and place back in the refrigerator for 10 to 15 minutes.

6   Remove from the refrigerator and add the final layer of buttercream. Frost with a smooth finish. This will allow the drip to run smoothly.

7   Set in the freezer for 15 to 20 minutes. The cake should be cold enough to help set the ganache.

8   Warm the ganache gently until you can pour it.

9   Pour ganache into a squeeze bottle with a nozzle top and create drips along the side of the cake.

10 Squeeze a large pool of ganache on the top centre of the cake. Use an offset spatula to evenly spread it, being careful not to push it over the edge, as it will ruin the perfect drips.

*Arrange the **chocolates** as you see fit, creating height and dimension to the top of the cake.*

If you like, you can cut them in halves or thirds and create a patterned border around the base. Place a few on the sides as well.

There really is no right or wrong to this cake.

Cupcake Assembly

1   Core each cupcake using an apple corer.

2   Place warmed ganache in a squeeze bottle.

3   Squeeze a little into each cupcake and insert a brownie piece.

4   Put the buttercream in a piping bag with a 1A tip, and pipe a semi-swirl.

5   Insert chocolate pieces and brownie chunks.

6   Drizzle with ganache.

I don't want to jinx it, but I think the luck of the Irish would be on your side if you showed up with this cake to your next Paddy's Day celebration.

This cake is a play on the drink the Dublin Drop, which is a glass of Guinness with a shot of Irish whiskey dropped in and chugged.

The silky-smooth Baileys Buttercream lusciously covers the bold Guinness cake.

ST. PATRICK'S DAY:
GUINNESS AND BAILEYS CAKE

1 batch of **Chocolate Cake batter,** Guinness substituted for the milk, divided evenly into two 8" gooped pans and baked

1½ batches of **Swiss Meringue Buttercream** plus ⅓ to ⅔ cup of **Baileys Irish Cream** or **Irish whiskey** to taste, divided into three, and coloured in three shades of green with gel food colour

½ cup **Simple Syrup** plus 3 to 4 Tbsp of **Guinness** (syrup not required for cupcakes)

½ pound of semi-firm semi-sweet **Chocolate Ganache, Baileys** substituted for half the heavy cream (ratio 1½:1)

Chocolate coins and twisted rainbow **candy ribbons** for decoration

Cake Assembly

1   Level and torte the cakes, giving you four layers.

2   Spread a small amount of buttercream onto the cake plate so the first layer of cake sticks to it.

3   Layer the cake as follows:

cake—soaked in syrup

one-third of the ganache, spread thinly

1 cup of Baileys buttercream (lightest green)

cake—soaked in syrup

one-third of the ganache, spread thinly

1 cup of Baileys buttercream (medium green)

cake—soaked in syrup

one-third of the ganache, spread thinly

1 cup of Baileys buttercream (darkest green)

cake—soaked in syrup

4   Place in the refrigerator for 15 to 20 minutes to set up before crumb-coating. This will help stabilize the cake and set the buttercream so the layers don't slide apart while finishing.

May the luck of the Irish be with you,
and may you enjoy it responsibly.

5   Crumb-coat the cake with a thin layer of buttercream and place back in the refrigerator for 10 to 15 minutes.

6   Remove from the refrigerator and add the final layer of buttercream. Frost with a smooth finish with an ombré effect.

→   Starting at the bottom of the cake, frost a little more than one-third of the cake with the darkest colour, then move up to the medium colour, then the lightest near the top edge and on the top of the cake.

→   When you use the bench scraper to smooth out the frosting, it will blend the colours together.

7   Place a line of chocolate coins and rainbow candies across the cake and cascading down the front of the cake.

Cupcake Assembly

1   Gently warm the ganache and dip the top of each cupcake into it. Allow it to set for a few minutes so the buttercream doesn't slide off (pop it in the freezer if you wish).

2   Place the three shades of green buttercream in separate tipless piping bags. Drop the three bags of buttercream down into a fourth bag with a 1M tip. When you start to squeeze, all three colours should begin to come out at the same time. Pipe a large swirl onto each cupcake.

3   Top with rainbow candy and chocolate coins.

I can't decide what's cuter, an Easter bonnet parade or this cake. This cake is a fun, playful funfetti cake, filled with a Mini-Egg buttercream and finished off with a cute, simple bunny . . . bum!

BURROWING BUNNY CAKE

1 batch of **Classic Vanilla Cake batter** plus ½ to ⅔ cup of **confetti sprinkles**, divided evenly into three 8" gooped pans and baked

1½ batches of **American Buttercream**, divided:

*To one-third of the batch, add ¼ cup crushed **Mini Eggs**.*

Leave the other two-thirds white for now.

For crushed Mini Eggs, place Mini Eggs in a food processor and pulverize to a fine powder, while being careful not to turn it into paste, as the chocolate will melt.

*For cupcakes only 1½ batches of **American Buttercream**, divided:*

Reserve 1½ cups white buttercream for bunny bums.

*Add ½ cup crushed **Mini Eggs** to remaining buttercream.*

½ cup **Simple Syrup** (not required for cupcakes)

Blue food colouring

1 to 1½ cups of **green shredded coconut** (page 131)

Extra **Mini Eggs** and **confetti sprinkles**, plus (optional) **carrot candies**

Cake Assembly

1 Level the cakes.

2 Spread a small amount of buttercream onto the cake plate so the first layer of cake sticks to it.

3 Layer the cake as follows:

> cake—soaked in syrup
>
> half of the Mini-Egg buttercream
>
> cake—soaked in syrup
>
> half of the Mini-Egg buttercream
>
> cake—soaked in syrup

4 Place in the refrigerator for 15 to 20 minutes to set before crumb-coating. This will help stabilize the cake and set the buttercream so the layers don't slide apart while finishing.

5 Crumb-coat the cake with a thin layer of the white buttercream and place back in the refrigerator for 10 to 15 minutes.

6 Remove from the refrigerator and add the final layer of white buttercream. Frost with a smooth finish. Frost the cake in white, as you normally would for a smooth cake, but adding a blue watercolour effect.

→ Take a small amount of buttercream (¼ cup will do) and turn it light blue by adding a few drops of blue food colouring.

→ Using an offset spatula, add little spots of blue frosting onto the white frosting, randomly around the cake.

→ Using the bench scraper, smooth the cake and the blue buttercream will spread out and blend with the white. You can always add more blue buttercream in some places and smooth it again.

7 Place sprinkles on the lower edge of the cake.

8 Sprinkle green coconut on top of the cake to look like grass.

9 For the bunny, place the white buttercream in a piping bag with 1A tip, and pipe a large blob in the centre of the cake. On top of that, pipe a smaller dollop—the tail—and allow it to set.

10 For the feet, starting away from the bum part, squeeze the piping bag and move towards the bum, slowly releasing pressure to create a teardrop shape. Do this twice.

11 Once the tail has set a little, use a toothpick to rough it up to make it look furry.

12 Use pink sprinkles for pads on the feet.

13 Randomly place the Mini Eggs around the cake. Little carrot candies would also be super sweet!

Cupcake Assembly

1 Place the Mini-Egg buttercream in a piping bag with 1M tip, and pipe a rosette on top of each cupcake.

2 Dip the top of the buttercream in green coconut for the grass.

3 Use the same technique as for the cake to create the bunny bums by piping reserved white buttercream, but substitute the smaller #12 tip for the 1A tip.

4 Place a Mini Egg or two on the cupcakes.

GREEN SHREDDED COCONUT

*Place **coconut** in a zipper bag and add 2 to 3 drops of **green gel colour**. Close bag, shake, and massage the green colour into the coconut until all coconut is coated. Add an additional drop or two of gel if needed.*

Every birthday celebration has cake. So why should Canada's birthday be any different? This fun little number is not only a party on the outside, it contains a fun little surprise on the inside: when you slice into this party cake, the flags should be staring back at you!

CANADA DAY CAKE

½ batch of **Classic Vanilla Cake batter**, **red food colouring** added, baked in a 9" x 13" pan, cooled, cut into maple-leaf shapes (using a two-inch maple-leaf cookie cutter)

If you're making cake, do this step first. If you're making cupcakes, skip this step and start with the Classic Vanilla Cake below.

....

1 batch of **Classic Vanilla Cake batter**, divided and coloured as follows:

To half of the batch, add red food colouring, and to the other half add white food colouring.

For cake, goop two 8" pans. Pour the red-coloured batter into one. To the other pan, add a little of the white-coloured batter (enough to cover the bottom). Then arrange the baked maple-leaf cut-outs (from above) in a circle around the edge, standing them upright. Pour the remaining batter in gently. Bake the cakes.

For cupcakes, layer the two batters into each lined cupcake cup, alternating between red and white. Bake.

....

½ cup **Simple Syrup** (not required for cupcakes)

....

1½ batches of **American Buttercream**, divided:

To one-quarter of the batch, add red food colouring. Leave the remainder white.

....

Variety of **candy** in red and white for decoration
Coloured Chocolate Shards (page 134) for decoration

Cake Assembly

1   Level all the cakes and torte the red cake, giving two layers.

2   Spread a small amount of buttercream onto the cake plate so the first layer of cake sticks to it.

3   Layer the cake as follows:

red cake—soaked in syrup
....
1 cup of white buttercream
....
white cake—soaked in syrup
....
1 cup of white buttercream
....
red cake—soaked in syrup

4   Place in the refrigerator for 15 to 20 minutes to set before crumb-coating. This will help stabilize the cake and set the buttercream so the layers don't slide apart while finishing.

5   Crumb-coat the cake with white buttercream and place back in the refrigerator for 10 to 15 minutes.

6   Remove from the refrigerator and add the final layer of buttercream. Frost with a smooth finish with red accents. Using a small offset spatula, take small dollops of red buttercream and swipe them randomly along the sides of the cake.

COLOURED CHOCOLATE SHARDS

*Melt half a cup each of **red-** and **white-coloured chocolate** or Candy Melts separately until smooth.*

Drop a small dollop onto parchment paper. Using the back of a spoon, drag the chocolate in a straight line across the paper.

Make 18 to 24 for cakes or two to three per cupcake.

Allow to set completely before removing from paper.

Cupcake Assembly

1   Place red and white buttercream in separate tipless piping bags. Drop the two bags into a third piping bag with a 1M tip.

2   Pipe a swirl on top of cupcakes.

3   Finish with candy and chocolate shards.

½ batch of **Classic Vanilla Cake batter**, **white food colouring** added, baked in a 9" x 13" pan, cooled, cut into maple-leaf shapes (using a two-inch star-shaped cookie cutter)

If you're making cake, do this step first. If you're making cupcakes, skip this step and start with the Classic Vanilla Cake below.

. . . .

1 batch of **Classic Vanilla Cake batter**, divided and coloured as follows:

To half of the batch, add red food colouring. To one-quarter of the batch, add white food colouring, and to the remaining quarter, add royal blue food colouring.

For cake, goop three 8" pans. Pour the red-coloured batter into one and the white-coloured batter into another. To the third pan, add a little of the blue-coloured batter (enough to cover the bottom). Then arrange the baked star-shaped cut-outs (from above) in a circle around the edge, standing them upright. Pour the remaining batter in gently. Bake the cakes.

For cupcakes, layer the three batters into each lined cupcake cup. Alternate between the red and white, and end with a layer of blue. Bake.

. . . .

½ cup **Simple Syrup** (not required for cupcakes)

. . . .

1½ batches of **American Buttercream**

For cake, colour ½ cup of the buttercream royal blue. Colour ½ cup of the buttercream red. Leave the remainder white.

For cupcakes, divide buttercream into thirds. Leave one white; colour one red and the last one blue.

. . . .

Variety of **candy** in red and white for decoration
Coloured Chocolate Shards (page 134) for decoration

This cake concept can easily be converted to help you celebrate your next Independence Day party.

INDEPENDENCE DAY CAKE

Cake Assembly

1 Level all the cakes and torte the red cake, giving you two layers of red.

2 Spread a small amount of buttercream onto the cake plate so the first layer of cake sticks to it.

3 Layer the cake as follows:

blue cake—soaked in syrup

1 cup of white buttercream

red cake—soaked in syrup

1 cup of white buttercream

white cake—soaked in syrup

1 cup of white buttercream

red cake—soaked in syrup

4 Place in the refrigerator for 15 to 20 minutes to set before crumb-coating. This will help stabilize the cake and set the buttercream so the layers don't slide apart while finishing.

5 Crumb-coat the cake with a thin layer of white buttercream and place back in the refrigerator for 10 to 15 minutes.

6 Remove from the refrigerator and add a final layer of white buttercream. Frost with a smooth finish with red accents: using a small offset spatula, take small dollops of red and blue buttercream and swipe them randomly along the sides of the cake.

7 Place various red, white, and blue candies on the cake. Use various heights and sizes to give the cake dimension. It's a party—have fun!

Cupcake Assembly

1 Place red, white, and blue buttercream in separate tipless piping bags. Drop the three bags into a fourth piping bag with a 1M tip.

2 Pipe a swirl on top of cupcakes.

3 Finish with candy and chocolate shards.

1 batch of **Chocolate Cake batter** plus 1 Tbsp of **black gel food colour**

*For cake, divide half of the batter evenly into three 8" gooped pans. Add **Orange Cake Pops**, pour the rest of the batter over them, and bake.*

For cupcakes, make 5 very small (about 1 tsp) cake pops per cupcake and freeze. Place half the required black cupcake batter into each liner. Place 3 cake pops in the batter; cover with remaining batter. Place two remaining pops on top of each cupcake. Bake.

½ cup **Simple Syrup** (not required for cupcakes)

1 batch of **American Buttercream**

Make this ahead because you'll need it for the Orange Cake Pops. Reserve ¼ cup uncoloured (white) buttercream for that purpose.

*If piping your spider (see below), reserve ¼ cup of buttercream and colour it using **black gel food colour**.*

*Use **purple gel food colouring** to colour the rest of the buttercream.*

1 batch **Pastry Cream, green and yellow gel food colour** added, cornstarch omitted, to make "slime."

note Instead of the Pastry Cream, you can use store-bought vanilla pudding and dye it green to make the "slime."

Marshmallow Spiderwebs (page 139) for decoration

Spider, a toy one, or pipe an edible one (page 141)

ORANGE CAKE POPS
Cake cut-offs (from levelling etc., or a few vanilla cupcakes baked and cooled)

orange food gel colour

a small amount of **buttercream**

The little ghouls and goblins will be screaming in fear when you take out this cake, covered in spiderwebs and a huge eight-legged critter! This black cake has a secret surprise of orange cake pops baked into it and is filled with a delicious green pudding.

HALLOWEEN:
WITCHES' BREW CAKE

To Make Orange Cake Pops

note You'll need to make these ahead and freeze them.

1   Crumble cake pieces in a bowl and add orange food gel colour, or colour of your choice. Add white buttercream a tablespoon at a time, as you don't want to make the cake pops too wet.

2   Mix thoroughly by hand, adding more buttercream as necessary, until you can form it into balls that hold together nicely when squeezed in your hand, but not so wet that they're sticky or mushy.

3   Make various sizes if being used for cake; make all of them small if being used for cupcakes. Freeze.

Cake Assembly

1   Level the cakes.

2   Spread a small amount of purple buttercream onto the cake plate so the first layer of cake sticks to it.

Freeze for later
Put the extra bits of cake cut off from other recipes in the freezer for using in cake pops.

MARSHMALLOW SPIDERWEBS

*You will need 2 cups of **mini marshmallows** and 1 Tbsp of **water**.*

Melt marshmallows in water, then set aside until cool to the touch.

note *Mini marshmallows melt more evenly and faster than larger ones.*

Warning: This gets messy, but it's the only way . . .

Once the cake is frosted and ready to be decorated, make the webs. With your hands, pick up some of the marshmallow and press both hands together and pull them apart. As the strings of marshmallow are created between your hands, wrap them around the cake.

Try various speeds of pulling to get various thicknesses of strands.

Repeat this process until you are happy with the webs.

3 Layer the cake as follows:

cake—soaked in syrup

....

purple buttercream, piped into a dam around the edge
(See Damming and Filling, page 15)

....

half of the pastry cream "slime" (about ½ cup), filled in the centre

....

cake—soaked in syrup

....

purple buttercream, piped into a dam around the edge

....

half of the pastry cream "slime" (about ½ cup), filled in the centre

....

cake—soaked in syrup

4 Place in the refrigerator for 25 to 30 minutes to set before crumb-coating. This will help stabilize the cake and set the buttercream so the layers don't slide apart while finishing.

5 Crumb-coat the cake with a thin layer of purple buttercream and place back in the refrigerator for 10 to 15 minutes.

6 Remove from the refrigerator and add the final layer of buttercream. Frost with a smooth finish so the spiderwebs stick nicely.

7 Finish with a Black Buttercream Spider (or a toy one) and Marshmallow Spiderwebs.

BLACK BUTTERCREAM SPIDER

Fill a piping bag with a #12 tip with **black buttercream**. *Pipe a large oval and then a smaller one attached, for the body and head.*

Fill a piping bag with #3 tip and pipe eight legs, four on each side.

Cupcake Assembly

1 Core each cupcake using an apple corer.

2 Place "slime" into a piping bag with no tip, and fill each cupcake.

3 Place purple buttercream in a piping bag with a 1A piping tip, and pipe a semi-swirl on top of each cupcake.

4 Decorate with a Black Buttercream Spider (or a toy one) and Marshmallow Spiderwebs.

String the lights and pass the eggnog! This cake is the perfect way to start any holiday decorating party. For this cake I took a couple of our favourite holiday decorating elements and packed in the eggnog flavour—and a splash of rum too, if you wish!

CHRISTMAS TREE CAKE

1 batch of **Classic Vanilla Cake batter, eggnog** substituted for the milk, divided evenly into three 8" gooped pans and baked

1½ batches of **American Buttercream, eggnog** substituted for the heavy cream, plus ½ tsp of ground **nutmeg**

*For cake, add **green gel food colour** to one-third of the buttercream and leave the rest uncoloured (white), reserving ¼ cup to colour with **black food gel**. (Food colour not required for cupcakes.)*

½ cup of **Simple Syrup** plus 2 Tbsp melted, unsalted **butter** and 3 to 4 Tbsp **dark rum** (optional)

Black Buttercream or shoe-string candy for decoration

Bag of **M&M's** for decoration

Pretzel Trees (page 144) for decoration

BLACK BUTTERCREAM
*To ¼ cup of the **white buttercream**, add 1 to 1½ tsp of **black food gel**.*

Mix until fully incorporated.

Cake Assembly

1   Level the cakes.

2   Spread a small amount of buttercream onto the board or cake plate to adhere to the first cake layer.

3   Layer the cake as follows:

cake—soaked in syrup

1 cup of white buttercream

cake—soaked in syrup

1 cup of white buttercream

cake—soaked in syrup

4   Place in the refrigerator for 15 to 20 minutes to set before crumb-coating. This will help stabilize the cake and set the buttercream so the layers don't slide apart while finishing.

5   Crumb-coat the cake with a thin layer of white buttercream and place back in the refrigerator for 10 to 15 minutes.

6   Remove from the refrigerator and add the final layer of white buttercream. Frost with a smooth finish and make green butter-cream trees for the side.

→   To create the trees, put the green buttercream in a piping bag with a #104 piping tip and follow the directions on page 143.

7   Pipe a string of black buttercream around the cake (or wrap the cake with black shoestring licorice). Press M&M's on their side into the cake to resemble a string of lights.

8   Carefully stand pretzel trees in the top of the cake.

BUTTERCREAM TREES

*Hold the bag parallel to the tabletop, with
the larger side of the piping tip towards the cake.*

*Squeeze piping bag, moving in an upward zigzag pattern that
becomes gradually smaller as you go up.*

Create varying widths and heights, but repeat all the way around the cake.

*Add your favourite **sprinkles**, same as on the Pretzel Trees.*

PRETZEL TREES

*Place **pretzel sticks** on a parchment-lined sheet such that they look like the branches of an evergreen tree.*

*Melt **green coating chocolate** (available at craft or cake supply stores), place it in a tipless piping bag, cut a small hole, and drizzle chocolate over pretzel sticks, starting wide at the base and going narrower as you make the tree taller.*

*Before the chocolate sets, sprinkle with your favourite **sprinkles**. I used rainbow nonpareils to resemble lights on the tree.*

Cupcake Assembly

note If using the rum butter syrup, brush the tops of cupcakes with it.

1 Place the white buttercream into a piping bag with a 1A tip, and pipe a blob onto each cupcake.

2 With the black buttercream, pipe a string onto each cupcake and place M&M's on their side next to the black string, to resemble tree lights.

3 Place a pretzel tree on top.

OUT-OF-THE-BOX FLAVOUR PAIRINGS

AND NO, I DON'T MEAN OUT OF THE CAKE BOX.

In this section, I wanted to feature some cake flavours that you may never have dreamed of or that surprise you.

These cakes have all been tried and tested . . . nothing to scare you here. In fact, they are popular flavour combinations that I am asked for often.

LEMON, PEPPER AND PARSLEY CAKE • PAGE 159

BEER AND CHEESE CAKE • PAGE 153

CARAMEL-CORN CAKE • PAGE 156

MAPLE BACON CAKE • PAGE 162

AVOCADO AND COFFEE CAKE
• PAGE 150

SPICY CHOCOLATE
CAKE • PAGE 165

Avocado is a neutral flavour but full of good fats. It lends itself nicely to be used in sweets because it will help carry some of the flavours while balancing them with its earthiness.

We've all seen the avocado chocolate pudding recipe going around so we know that avocado and chocolate pair well together.

Another great pair is chocolate and coffee. Coffee is a great way to enhance chocolate flavour in a recipe.

AVOCADO AND COFFEE CAKE

1 batch of **Chocolate Cake batter**, with double the strength of the coffee, divided evenly into three 8" gooped pans and baked

1½ batches of **American Buttercream** plus 2 very ripe, puréed **avocados**

½ cup **Simple Syrup** plus 1 Tbsp **instant coffee** dissolved in 1 tsp **hot water**

Candy pearl sprinkles for decoration (use green to match the theme)

Cake Assembly

1   Level the cakes.

2   Spread a small amount of buttercream onto the cake plate so the first layer of cake sticks to it.

3   Layer the cake as follows:

cake—soaked in syrup
....
1 cup of buttercream
....
cake—soaked in syrup
....
1 cup of buttercream
....
cake—soaked in syrup

4   Place in the refrigerator for 15 to 20 minutes to set before crumb-coating. This will help stabilize the cake and set the buttercream so the layers don't slide apart while finishing.

5   Crumb-coat the cake with a thin layer of buttercream and place back in the refrigerator for 10 to 15 minutes.

6   Remove from the refrigerator and add the final layer of butter-cream. Frost with a petal finish (see Petal Piping, page 20), leaving the top smooth.

7   Decorate the outer edge with sprinkles.

Cupcake Assembly

1   Brush each cupcake with the syrup.

2   Place the buttercream in a piping bag with a 1A piping tip, and pipe teardrops around the edge of the cupcake. Release the pressure on the piping bag as you move towards the centre of the cupcake. Add a few dollops on top to fill in the centre.

3   Sprinkle with candy pearl sprinkles.

This cake is a beer lover's dream. It starts with a nice pale ale (use your favourite), baked in vanilla cake so that the flavour really shines. The aged cheddar can be found not only in the cake but also in the cream cheese frosting. But in case that wasn't enough, there's bacon too!

The sweet, salty, and savoury elements all come together in a beautiful marriage to create the perfect bite.

This cake would be the perfect treat for your next tailgate party or Super-bowl Sunday treat.

BEER AND CHEESE CAKE

1 batch of **Classic Vanilla Cake batter**, oil reduced to ¾ cup, **pale ale** substituted for the milk, plus the following ingredients, the resulting batter divided evenly into two 8" gooped pans and baked

¼ cup **sour cream**

½ cup of grated **aged cheddar**

⅓ cup **bacon**, finely crumbled

1 Tbsp **bacon fat**

½ cup **Simple Syrup** plus 3 to 4 Tbsp **pale ale**

1½ batches of **Cream Cheese Frosting** plus ½ cup of cooked **bacon**, finely crumbled in a food processor; and ½ cup grated **aged cheddar**

Maple Candied Bacon (page 163) (optional)

Cake Assembly

1   Level the cakes.

2   Spread a small amount of frosting onto the cake plate so the first layer of cake sticks to it.

3   Layer the cake as follows:

cake—soaked in syrup

1 cup of frosting

cake—soaked in syrup

1 cup of frosting

cake—soaked in syrup

1 cup of frosting

cake—soaked in syrup

4   Place in the refrigerator for 15 to 20 minutes to set before crumb-coating. This will help stabilize the cake and set the frosting so the layers don't slide apart while finishing.

5   Crumb-coat the cake with a thin layer of frosting and place back in the refrigerator for 10 to 15 minutes.

Get the perfect scoop!
Dip the scoop into hot water
between each scoop. It will give
you perfect scoops each time.

6   Remove from the refrigerator and add a final layer of frosting, reserving some to scoop on top for decoration. The finish will not be perfectly smooth because of the bacon and cheese.

7   Warm your purple scoop in a glass of hot water. Place scoops of frosting around the top of the cake.

8   Decorate with maple candied bacon (if using).

Cupcake Assembly

1   Brush the top of each cupcake with syrup.

2   Warm your red scoop in a glass of hot water. Place scoops of the frosting on top of each cupcake.

3   Decorate with maple candied bacon (if using).

Of all the carnival snacks out there, this one is my favourite, hands down. It's the perfect balance of sweet and salty, crunchy, and a little chewy from the caramel. This cake embodies the whole flavour balance in each bite.

CARAMEL-CORN CAKE

1 batch of **Classic Vanilla Cake batter**, plus ¼ cup **sour cream**, with ⅓ cup of the flour replaced by ¼ cup **cornmeal**, divided evenly into three 8" gooped pans and baked

1½ batches of **American Buttercream** plus ¾ cup **Caramel Sauce**

½ cup **Simple Syrup** plus ¼ cup **Caramel Sauce** (syrup not required for cupcakes)

2 batches of **Caramel Sauce**

Caramel corn for decoration (I just buy my favourite)

Cake Assembly

1   Level the cakes.

2   Spread a small amount of buttercream onto the cake plate so the first layer of cake sticks to it.

3   Layer the cake as follows:

cake—soaked in syrup

1 cup buttercream

half of the caramel sauce, drizzled

cake—soaked in syrup

1 cup buttercream

half of the caramel sauce, drizzled

cake—soaked in syrup

4   Place in the refrigerator for 15 to 20 minutes to set before crumb-coating. This will help stabilize the cake and set the buttercream so the layers don't slide apart while finishing.

5   Crumb-coat the cake with a thin layer of buttercream and place back in the refrigerator for 10 to 15 minutes.

6   Remove from the refrigerator, and add a final layer of buttercream. Frost with a lightly roughed-up buttercream texture, reserving a small amount for the next step.

7   Place a pile of caramel corn on top and a large cascade of caramel corn on the side of the cake. Use extra buttercream to hold the corn together as you pile it on.

Cupcake Assembly

1 Core each cupcake using an apple corer.

2 Place the caramel sauce in a piping bag with no tip and fill each cupcake.

3 Place the buttercream in a piping bag fitted with a 1A tip, and pipe a large swirl on top.

4 Decorate with your favourite caramel corn.

1 batch of **Classic Vanilla Cake batter**, with **Parsley- and Peppercorn-Infused Milk** substituted for the milk

*Colour the batter with **green food colouring** and pour it evenly into two 8" gooped pans, OR, for more drama, divide it into quarters, make each quarter a different shade of green, and pour it into four 8" gooped pans. Bake.*

1 batch of **American Buttercream** adjusted as follows:

*Substitute the cream with ½ cup Simple Syrup that has been thoroughly blended with parsley and peppercorns left over from **Parsley- and Peppercorn-Infused Milk** (below).*

½ cup **Simple Syrup** plus the parsley and peppercorns left over from the infused milk (below), well blended

2 batches **Lemon Curd** plus 2 tsp crushed **pink and white peppercorns**

PARSLEY- AND PEPPERCORN-INFUSED MILK

1 cup of **milk**

¾ cup of chopped **parsley**

½ Tbsp of roughly smashed **pink and white peppercorns**

Simmer the milk, parsley, and peppercorns for 10 minutes and strain. Keep parsley and peppercorns for use in the Simple Syrup.

*note Simmering milk with the parsley and peppercorns will infuse the milk with the flavours. Do not boil, or else you will end up with a **huge** mess.*

This is the favourite cake of Aimee, the photographer.

I was lucky enough to compete on Food Network's *Spring Baking Championship* against against nine incredibly talented bakers—now friends for life. We were challenged to create a naked ombré cake that incorporated a fresh herb chosen for us. They gave me *parsley*! And to my surprise—I won that challenge!

Parsley has a slight pepper taste and pairs nicely with lemon, and pepper also pairs with lemon, so here we go.

LEMON, PEPPER AND PARSLEY CAKE

Cake Assembly

1   Level the cakes (if you made four) or level and torte the cakes (if you made two), giving you four layers.

2   Spread a small amount of buttercream onto the cake plate so the first layer of cake sticks to it.

3   Layer the cake as follows:

cake—soaked in syrup

buttercream, dollops piped around the edge and a large dollop in the centre

one-quarter of the lemon curd, filled in

cake—soaked in syrup

buttercream, dollops piped around the edge and a large dollop in the centre

one-quarter of the lemon curd, filled in

cake—soaked in syrup

buttercream, dollops piped around the edge, and a large dollop in the centre

one-quarter of the lemon curd, filled in

cake—soaked in syrup

On the show, I created some **chocolate spheres** for the top that I did not include here. However, you can find a tutorial for them on my YouTube channel: www.youtube.com/manversuscake

note The decoration on the top of this cake was piped with a #22 tip.

4   Place in the refrigerator for 25 to 30 minutes to set before finishing the cake. This will help stabilize the cake and set the buttercream so the layers don't slide apart while finishing.

5   Pipe a buttercream border on the top edge of the cake and put another layer of lemon curd on the top of the cake.

6   Leave the cake as is—this is a naked cake!

Cupcake Assembly

1   Brush each cupcake with the syrup.

2   Place the buttercream in a piping bag with a 6B piping tip, and pipe a nest on each cupcake.

3   Place the curd in a piping bag, cut the tip off the bag, and fill the nest with the curd.

For as long as I can remember, I have *always* added maple syrup to bacon. It really comes back to that sweet and salty balance.

This cake is a moist maple cake that has flecks of real bacon throughout and is smothered in a maple buttercream. With, of course, more bacon on it! Candied bacon at that!

1 batch of **Classic Vanilla Cake batter,** plus the following ingredients, divided evenly into two 8" gooped pans and baked

1 Tbsp **maple flavouring**

½ cup cooked, crumbled **bacon**

3 Tbsp **bacon fat**

1½ batches of **Swiss Meringue Buttercream** plus 1½ Tbsp **maple flavouring**

½ cup of **Simple Syrup** (not required for cupcakes)

Maple Candied Bacon (page 163) for decoration

MAPLE BACON CAKE

Cake Assembly

1   Level and torte the cakes, giving you four layers.

2   Spread a small amount of buttercream onto the cake plate so the first layer of cake sticks to it.

3   Layer the cake as follows:

cake—soaked in syrup

1 cup of buttercream

cake—soaked in syrup

1 cup of buttercream

cake—soaked in syrup

1 cup of buttercream

cake—soaked in syrup

4   Place in the refrigerator for 25 to 30 minutes to set before finishing the cake. This will help stabilize the cake and set the buttercream so the layers don't slide apart while finishing.

5   Crumb-coat the cake with a thin layer of buttercream and place back in the refrigerator for 10 to 15 minutes.

6   Remove from the refrigerator and add the final layer of buttercream. Frost with a smooth finish.

MAPLE CANDIED BACON

*You will need ⅓ cup of **real maple syrup**, ½ cup **brown sugar**, ¼ tsp ground **cinnamon**, 1 lb of **bacon**, and extra **brown sugar** for finishing.*

Preheat oven to 400°F.

In a bowl, mix the syrup, sugar, and cinnamon.

Dip the bacon into the syrup mixture and coat both sides.

Place a single layer of bacon on a wire rack on top of a lined baking sheet, and sprinkle the bacon with a little extra brown sugar.

Bake for 15 minutes.

Turn the bacon over and sprinkle with more brown sugar. Bake for an additional 15 minutes.

Check for crispiness. Continue baking, checking every five minutes, until the bacon has the desired crispiness.

7   Break some of the candied bacon into pieces of various lengths and arrange them on top of the cake.

8   Crumble the remaining bacon, place it around the bottom edge of the cake and use a little on the top.

Cupcake Assembly

1   Place the buttercream in a piping bag with a 1A tip, and pipe a semi-swirl on top of the cupcake.

2   Break the candied bacon into pieces and place one on top of each cupcake.

3   Drizzle with additional maple syrup if you wish.

This cake is not for the faint of heart—I drew inspiration from Mexican chocolate, known for its perfect balance of spiciness and sweetness.

Sometimes it's hard to find some of the fresh fruits we want.
I went looking for a few items at the supermarket and couldn't find them, so I made some adjustments on the fly!

SPICY CHOCOLATE CAKE

1 batch of **Chocolate Cake batter**, plus the following ingredients, divided into three 8" pans and baked

1½ tsp **cinnamon**

1 tsp **cayenne**

1 tsp fresh **ginger**

½ tsp **allspice**

....

3 lbs semi-firm **Dark-Chocolate Ganache** (ratio 1½:1)

½ cup **Simple Syrup**
(not required for cupcakes)

1 batch of **Habanero Jam**
(page 166)

Fresh **figs** and **pears**, cut into wedges for decoration
(not required for cupcakes)

Apricot jam, store-bought, warmed for glazing
(not required for cupcakes)

Cake Assembly

1   Level the cakes.

2   Spread a small amount of ganache onto the cake plate so the first layer of cake sticks to it.

3   Layer the cake as follows:

cake—soaked in syrup
....
¾ cup ganache
....
¼ cup habanero jam, spread thinly
....
cake—soaked in syrup
....
¾ cup ganache
....
¼ cup habanero jam, spread thinly
....
cake—soaked in syrup

4   Place in the refrigerator for 15 to 20 minutes to set before crumb-coating. This will help stabilize the cake and set the ganache so the layers don't slide apart while finishing.

5   Crumb-coat the cake with a thin layer of ganache and place it back in the refrigerator for 10 to 15 minutes.

Slow down the brown   *Glazing the fruit will help slow the oxidization (turning brown) and give a shine that will make the fruit look more appealing.*

HABANERO JAM

*You will need 6 fresh **figs**, quartered, 1 **habanero chili**, finely diced, 1 firm **pear**, peeled and roughly chopped, ½ cup **apricot jam**, 3 Tbsp **sugar**, and a pinch of **salt**.*

Place everything in a pot and cook over medium heat until the fruit becomes tender and begins to break down, and there are few large chunks remaining. Allow to cool completely before using.

note For a spicy hot jam, leave the chili seeds in. For medium spiciness, remove them. For a milder jam, use a chili milder than a habanero.

6   Remove from the refrigerator and add the final layer of ganache. Frost with a smooth finish to really highlight the fruit.

7   Arrange the fruit on top of the cake and glaze with warmed apricot jam. Place dollops of remaining habanero jam in and around the fruit.

Cupcake Assembly

1   Warm the ganache and dip the top of each cupcake in it.

2   Warm the remaining ganache and put it in a piping bag with a #12 tip. Pipe a nest around the edge of each cupcake.

3   Put the habanero jam in another piping bag, cut a small hole in the tip of the bag, and fill the nest.

SEASONAL

FLAVOURS

THIS SECTION OF THE BOOK IS ALL ABOUT THE FLAVOURS OF THE SEASON.

We've tackled holidays, but these cakes are less about fitting into a party theme and more about seasonal taste.

There are only certain times of year when we can get certain fruits, or when spices are more readily welcomed. Summer sunshine makes us think of bright, cheerful, inviting flavours; fall just makes us want to curl up with a blanket and sip warm cider.

For every season, I bring you two cakes that explode with seasonal flavours.

STRAWBERRY BASIL SHORTCAKE • PAGE 172

PEACH-AND-BLACKBERRY-STREUSEL CAKE • PAGE 179

STICKY-TOFFEE-PUDDING CAKE • PAGE 197

CRANBERRY-CRUMBLE CAKE PAGE 194

LEMON, LAVENDER AND ROSEMARY CAKE • PAGE 176

PECAN PIECAKEN • PAGE 190

PUMPKIN-PIE CAKE • PAGE 186

PINK LEMONADE CAKE • PAGE 182

When I was growing up, strawberry shortcake was a staple in late spring and through the summer.

We would berry-pick for hours and hours with Mom, bringing home enough to get us through the year. After spending a day at the u-pick, we would spend another day cleaning, chopping, and preparing berries for the freezer.

This cake is truly a mouthful of flavour. A hint of cardamom gives it a little citrus and floral note to elevate the freshness of the strawberries. Basil—peppery and floral—lends itself beautifully to the berries and the spice cake.

SPRING:
STRAWBERRY BASIL SHORTCAKE

1 batch of **Classic Vanilla Cake batter** plus 2½ tsp ground **cardamom**, divided evenly into three 8" gooped pans and baked

½ batch of **Swiss Meringue Buttercream**

½ cup **Simple Syrup** (not required for cupcakes)

2 batches of **Fruit Filling** (use strawberries) plus 2 Tbsp finely chopped **basil**, added after removing filling from heat

Fresh **strawberries** for decoration, halved for cake, or sliced for cupcakes

Mini Biscuits (page 173) for decoration

Cake Assembly

1   Level the cakes.

2   Spread a small amount of buttercream onto the cake plate so the first layer of cake sticks to it.

3   Layer the cake as follows:

cake—soaked in syrup

buttercream, spread thinly to act as a moisture barrier

buttercream, dollops piped into a dam around the edge and a large dollop in the centre (See Damming and Filling, page 15)

one-third of the fruit filling, filled in the centre

cake—soaked in syrup

buttercream, spread thinly to act as a moisture barrier

buttercream, dollops piped into a dam around the edge and a large dollop in the centre

one-third of the fruit filling, filled in the centre

cake—soaked in syrup

4   Place in the refrigerator for 25 to 30 minutes to set before finishing the cake.

MINI BISCUITS

You will need 3 cups all-purpose **flour**, *¾ cup granulated* **sugar**, *2 Tbsp* **baking powder**, *½ tsp ground* **cardamom**, *a pinch of* **salt**, *¾ cup unsalted* **butter**, *cold, cubed, 1 large* **egg**, *and ¾ cup* **milk**.

Mix the flour, sugar, baking powder, cardamom, and salt in a bowl.

Cut the butter into the flour mixture.

In a small bowl, gently beat egg and milk together. Add to the flour mixture. Stir gently by hand just until the dough comes together; do not overmix.

Dust a thin layer of flour onto the countertop and drop the dough onto it. With your hands, press out the dough until about ½" thick. Using a cookie cutter, cut into 1" to 1¼" rounds.

Bake at 350°F for 15 to 18 minutes.

A slice of spring

There is nothing better than a little strawberry shortcake to round off a great BBQ or enjoy a slice with your favourite sweet tea!

5   Spread a thin layer of buttercream to act as a moisture barrier on the top, pipe swirls around the top edge of the cake to act as a dam, and put another layer of fruit filling on the top of the cake.

6   Leave the cake unfrosted—this is a naked cake. Place strawberries and biscuits around the top edge of the cake, alternating them as you go around.

Cupcake Assembly

1   Core each cupcake using an apple corer.

2   Place the fruit filling in a piping bag with no tip, and fill each cupcake.

3   Place the buttercream in a piping bag with a 6B piping tip, and pipe a half-swirl on each cupcake.

4   Top with a slice of strawberry and a biscuit.

I know what you're thinking. Lavender . . .

The key to using lavender is using very little. Overdoing it will land you with a cake that tastes like soap. Lavender pairs surprisingly well in savoury dishes, so bringing hints of fresh rosemary into the lemon cake helps bridge the gap between sweet and savoury.

SPRING:
LEMON, LAVENDER AND ROSEMARY CAKE

1 batch of **Classic Vanilla Cake batter**, plus the following ingredients, divided evenly into two 8" gooped pans and baked

Zest of 2 **lemons**

Juice of 1 **lemon**

1 Tbsp of **lemon extract** (or lemon emulsion)

2 tsp of **citric acid** (optional)

note Adding the citric acid will enhance the citrus flavour and make the cake slightly sour, cutting some of the sweetness.

1½ Tbsp finely chopped fresh **rosemary**

2 drops of **yellow gel food colour**

....

1 batch of **American Buttercream** plus 2 tsp of roughly ground dried **lavender** and 3 to 4 drops of **purple gel food colour**

½ cup of **Simple Syrup** (not required for cupcakes)

2 batches of **Lemon Curd**

Cake Assembly

1   Level and torte the cakes, giving you four layers.

2   Spread a small amount of buttercream onto the cake plate so the first layer of cake sticks to it.

3   Layer the cake as follows:

cake—soaked in syrup

buttercream, piped into a dam around the edge (See Damming and Filling, page 15)

one-third of the lemon curd, filled in the centre

cake—soaked in syrup

buttercream, piped into a dam around the edge

one-third of the lemon curd, filled in the centre

cake—soaked in syrup

buttercream, piped into a dam around the edge

one-third of the lemon curd, filled in the centre

cake—soaked in syrup

4   Place in the refrigerator for 15 to 20 minutes to set before crumb-coating. This will help stabilize the cake and set the buttercream so the layers don't slide apart while finishing.

Cooking and baking are all about striking the balance between sweet, salty, bitter, and sour. Lemons have a wonderful way of addressing both the sour and bitter!

5   Crumb-coat the cake with a thin layer of buttercream and place back in the refrigerator for 10 to 15 minutes.

6   Remove from the refrigerator and add another layer of buttercream. Frost with a smooth buttercream, reserving some for the next step.

7   Place the remaining buttercream in a bag with a 6B tip, and pipe swirls around the top edge of the cake.

There is something to be said about a simple finish on a cake. So classy, so elegant, and so perfect.

Cupcake Assembly

1   Core each cupcake using an apple corer.

2   Place the lemon curd in a piping bag with no tip, and fill each cupcake.

3   Place the buttercream in piping bag with a 6B piping tip, and pipe a swirl onto each cupcake.

Streusel is one of my favourite ways to use up fruit that may be a little past ripe. Apple is my all-time favourite, but . . .

Peaches have this wonderful way of getting sweeter as they ripen, so the softer they are, the sweeter they become. The addition of the blackberries is a great way to help balance that sweet flavour.

Don't cook the berries into the filling because you would lose the taste and because of the colour they would turn the filling!

1 batch of **Classic Vanilla Cake batter**, divided evenly into three 8" gooped pans and baked

1 batch of **Cream Cheese Frosting**

½ cup **Simple Syrup** (not required for cupcakes)

1 batch **Fruit Filling**, using 2 cups of peeled chopped **peaches** and ⅔ of a cup of **blackberries** (added after removing peaches from heat, while filling is still warm)

Baked Streusel (page 181)

Extra **blackberries** and **peach slices** for decoration, fresh or frozen

SUMMER:
PEACH-AND-BLACKBERRY-STREUSEL CAKE

Cake Assembly

1 Level the cakes.

2 Spread a small amount of frosting onto the cake plate so the first layer of cake sticks to it.

3 Layer the cake as follows:

cake—soaked in syrup

frosting, piped into a dam around the edge (See Damming and Filling, page 15)

half of the fruit filling, filled in the centre

cake—soaked in syrup

frosting, piped into a dam around the edge

half of the fruit filling, filled in the centre

cake—soaked in syrup

4 Place in the refrigerator for 15 to 20 minutes to set before crumb-coating. This will help stabilize the cake and set the frosting so the layers don't slide apart while finishing.

5 Crumb-coat the cake with a thin layer of frosting and place back in the refrigerator for 10 to 15 minutes.

BAKED STREUSEL

*You will need 1 cup all-purpose **flour**, ½ cup packed **brown sugar**, 1 tsp ground **cinnamon**, ¼ tsp **salt**, and ½ cup unsalted **butter**, cold and cubed.*

Place the flour, brown sugar, cinnamon, and salt in a bowl and mix.

Cut the butter into the flour mixture until it is crumbly and has pea-sized butter chunks.

Spread the mixture onto baking sheet and bake at 350°F for 10 to 12 minutes, until golden.

Crush to a semi-fine crumb, and allow to cool before using.

6 Remove from the refrigerator and add a final layer of frosting, reserving some for step 8. Frost with a smooth finish, but don't be too particular.

7 Press the streusel onto the top and sides of cake.

8 Place the frosting in a bag with a 1A tip, and pipe dollops around the top edge of the cake.

9 Decorate with blackberries and peach slices, alternating.

Cupcake Assembly

1 Core each cupcake using an apple corer.

2 Place the fruit filling in a piping bag with no tip, and fill each cupcake.

3 Place the remaining frosting in a piping bag with a 1A piping tip, and pipe a blob onto each cupcake.

4 Dip the cupcake in a bowl filled with streusel mix.

5 Top with a dollop of frosting and a piece of fruit.

This cake will have you dreaming of summer days, picnics, and cold lemonade. The sweet lemon cake is layered with the tart pink lemonade and a fresh raspberry surprise to help balance everything out.

For the adults, it's been kicked up a notch with a Limoncello simple syrup.

PINK LEMONADE CAKE

1 batch of **Classic Vanilla Cake batter**, plus the following ingredients, divided into three 8" gooped pans and baked

Zest of 2 **lemons**

Juice of 1 **lemon**

1 Tbsp of **lemon extract** (or lemon emulsion)

2 tsp of **citric acid** (optional)

note Adding the citric acid will enhance the citrus flavour and cut some of the sweetness.

2 drops of **yellow gel food colour**

1½ batches of **American Buttercream**, divided in one-third and two-thirds respectively (one-third pink, two-thirds yellow)

*To the first third, add 3 Tbsp of **pink lemonade juice crystals** dissolved in 2 to 3 tsp of **warm water** and 2 to 3 drops of **pink gel food colour** (for filling).*

*To the remaining two-thirds, add 2 Tbsp **lemon flavouring** and 2 to 3 drops of **yellow gel food colour** (for frosting).*

½ cup of **Simple Syrup** plus 3 to 4 Tbsp of **Limoncello** (optional)

½ pint of fresh **raspberries**, sliced in half for cake, or chopped for cupcakes

1 batch of **Pink Drip** (page 184)

Yellow and pink candy and **sprinkles** for decoration

Cake Assembly

1 Level and torte the cakes, giving you six layers.

2 Spread a small amount of buttercream onto the cake plate so the first layer of cake sticks to it.

3 Layer the cake as follows:

cake—soaked in syrup

¾ cup of pink buttercream

raspberries, handful

cake—soaked in syrup

¾ cup of pink buttercream

raspberries, handful

cake—soaked in syrup

¾ cup of pink buttercream

raspberries, handful

cake—soaked in syrup

¾ cup of pink buttercream

raspberries, handful

cake—soaked in syrup

¾ cup of pink buttercream

raspberries, handful

cake—soaked in syrup

When life hands you
lemons, skip the lemonade
and go straight for the cake!

4   Place in the refrigerator for 15 to 20 minutes to set before crumb-coating. This will help stabilize the cake and set the buttercream so the layers don't slide apart while finishing.

5   Crumb-coat the cake with a thin layer of yellow buttercream and place back in the refrigerator for 10 to 15 minutes.

6   Remove from the refrigerator and add the final layer of yellow buttercream. Frost with a smooth finish.

7   Set the frosted cake in the freezer for 15 to 20 minutes. The cake should be cold enough to help set the pink drip when added.

8   Warm the pink drip gently, until you can pour it into a squeeze bottle with a nozzle top.

9   First, create drips down the sides of the cake.

PINK DRIP

*You will need 10 oz of store-bought **pink coating chocolate** (available at craft or cake supply stores) and 2 oz of **water**.*

Melt the chocolate and mix with the water until smooth. Allow it to cool until it's not hot but still runny.

note You do not want a hot pink drip—it will drip to the bottom of the cake. If it is too warm, allow it to rest on the counter until it cools to room temperature.

10   Squeeze a large pool of pink drip on the top of the cake. Use an offset spatula to evenly spread it, being careful not to push it over the edge, as it will ruin the perfect drips.

11   Place an array of pink and yellow treats in a crescent moon pattern until you are happy.

12   Place some yellow sprinkles on the bottom edge of the cake.

Cupake Assembly

1   Brush the tops of the cupcakes with syrup.

2   Core each cupcake using an apple corer.

3   Fill the hole with chopped raspberries. If they are slightly macerated—that's perfect!

4   Place the pink and lemon buttercreams in separate piping bags with 1A piping tips.

5   First, pipe a rosette of pink lemonade buttercream.

6   Then pipe a blob of lemon buttercream.

7   Place pink drip in a squeeze bottle, and gently squeeze over the top
     of the buttercream.

8   Top with your favourite lemon candy.

Pumpkin-pie spice . . . need I say more? Autumn seems to be a favourite time of year for a lot of people, for many reasons—the beautiful colours, the smells in the air, and of course the *spices*.

Baking with spices is always sensational. The amazing aromas that fill the house and the delicious treats that ensue are enough to convince me it's the best time of year.

This cake will surely get you in the mood for fall. Moist chocolate cake, filled with a pumpkin-pie pudding and smothered in a pumpkin-pie spice buttercream and mini slices of pumpkin pie.

1 batch of **Chocolate Cake batter**, divided evenly into three 8" gooped pans and baked

1 batch of **American Buttercream** plus 2 Tbsp **Pumpkin-Pie Spice** (page 187)
For a latte taste, add 1½ tsp dissolved **espresso powder**.

½ cup **Simple Syrup** plus 3 to 4 Tbsp of **bourbon** or your favourite Canadian whisky (optional)
For a latte taste, replace the bourbon with 2 tsp dissolved **espresso powder**.

1 batch **Pumpkin-Pie Pudding**

Pumpkin pie (store-bought or homemade; I use the E.D. Smith recipe), cut into mini slices

1 batch of **Caramel Sauce**, for decoration

PUMPKIN-PIE PUDDING

1 can (15 oz) pure **pumpkin purée**

1 can (15 oz) of **evaporated milk**

1 large box (5.1 oz) **instant vanilla pudding**

1 Tbsp **Pumpkin-Pie Spice**

⅛ tsp **salt**

Place all ingredients in a bowl and whisk until smooth. Set in the refrigerator to chill for a couple of hours.

FALL:
PUMPKIN-PIE CAKE

Cake Assembly

1 Level the cakes.

2 Spread a small amount of buttercream onto the cake plate so the first layer of cake sticks to it.

3 Layer the cake as follows:

cake—soaked in syrup

buttercream, piped into a dam around the edge (See Damming and Filling, page 15)

half of the pudding, filled in the centre

cake—soaked in syrup

buttercream, piped into a dam around the edge

half of the pudding, filled in the centre

cake—soaked in syrup

4 Place in the refrigerator for 15 to 20 minutes to set before crumb-coating. This will help stabilize the cake and set the buttercream so the layers don't slide apart while finishing.

PUMPKIN-PIE SPICE

You will need 3 Tbsp ground cinnamon, 2 tsp ground ginger, 2 tsp ground nutmeg, 1½ tsp ground allspice, 1½ tsp ground cloves.

Place all spices in a bowl and mix well. Keep in an airtight container.

note Double or triple this and throw the extra in the cupboard.

5   Crumb-coat the cake with a thin layer of buttercream and place back in the refrigerator for 10 to 15 minutes.

6   Remove from the refrigerator and add the final layer of buttercream, reserving some for the next step. Frost with a smooth finish and carve a diagonal line pattern.

7   Place the remaining buttercream in a piping bag with a 1M piping tip and pipe rosettes around the top edge of the cake.

8   Place a mini slice of pumpkin pie in the middle of every other rosette.

9   Drizzle the top with caramel sauce.

Cupcake Assembly

1   Brush tops of cupcakes with syrup.

2   Core each cupcake using an apple corer.

3   Place the pudding in a piping bag with no tip, and fill the cupcake.

4   Place the buttercream in a piping bag with a 1M piping tip, and pipe a rosette on top of each cupcake.

5   Place a mini slice of pumpkin pie in the middle of the rosette.

6   Drizzle the top with caramel sauce.

2 **Pecan Pies**, store-bought or recipe below, removed from pie pans and placed into the **Chocolate Cake batter** as described

1 batch of **Chocolate Cake batter**, divided as follows:

For cake, goop two cake pans (8" round by 3" tall). Pour a small amount of batter (about 1") into each pan. Lay a pecan pie on top, pour in the rest of the batter, and bake.

note Most pies are nine inches. You can cut the outer crust off to fit the pie in the cake pan.

For cupcakes, chop the pecan pies into 1" chunks, and place two chunks in each lined cupcake cup. Scoop the batter over the pie chunks and bake.

1 batch of **American Buttercream** plus 1½ cups of **cocoa powder** and enough **milk** or heavy cream to make the buttercream spreadable

½ cup **Simple Syrup** (not required for cupcakes)

Toasted pecans and **Toasted Pecan Brittle** (page 191) for decoration

PECAN PIE
4 large **eggs**

1 cup packed **brown sugar**

1 cup **corn syrup**

½ cup unsalted **butter**, melted

1 tsp **vanilla**

½ tsp **salt**

3 cups toasted **pecan halves**

2 frozen deep-dish **pie shells**

Is it a pie? A cake? Pecan pies baked into the cake itself!

You can use store-bought pecan pies, but I've provided you with the recipe in case you would like to make one from scratch. And the brittle on top is a tasty treat.

FALL:
PECAN PIECAKEN

To Make Pecan Pie

1   Preheat the oven to 350°F.

2   Place the eggs, brown sugar, corn syrup, butter, vanilla, and salt in a bowl. Mix until the custard is smooth.

3   Place half of the pecan halves in each pie shell and add the custard.

4   Place the pies on a cookie sheet and bake for 60 to 70 minutes. The pie is done when the centre springs back and the custard is set.

5   Allow pies to cool completely before using for the cake.

Cake Assembly

1   Level the cakes.

2   Spread a small amount of buttercream onto the cake plate so the first layer of cake sticks to it.

3   Layer the cake as follows:

cake—soaked in syrup

1 cup of chocolate buttercream

cake—soaked in syrup

4   Place in the refrigerator for 15 to 20 minutes to set before crumb-coating. This will help stabilize the cake and set the buttercream so the layers don't slide apart while finishing.

TOASTED PECAN BRITTLE

You will need 1 cup granulated **sugar**, *½ cup* **light corn syrup**, *1 Tbsp unsalted* **butter**, *1 tsp* **vanilla**, *¼ tsp* **salt**, *1½ cups of toasted* **pecans**, *and 1 tsp* **baking soda**.

Preheat oven to 350°F.

Warm a silicone baking sheet on a metal baking sheet in the oven. This will help the brittle spread when poured.

Combine the sugar and corn syrup and heat gently, stirring.

Add the butter and keep heating until the mixture has an amber colour.

Add the vanilla, salt, and pecans, and keep heating until desired colour is reached.

Add the baking soda and stir to incorporate.

note Be careful when you add the baking soda, as the mixture will bubble. Do not overmix as you will lose the air.

Pour out onto the warmed silicone baking sheet, and allow to cool completely.

Break into pieces.

5   Crumb-coat the cake with a thin layer of buttercream and place back in the refrigerator for 10 to 15 minutes.

6   Remove from the refrigerator and add the final layer of buttercream, reserving a little bit for decorating. Frost with a rough texture.

→   Frost the cake as you would for a smooth finish.

→   Then take an offset spatula or the back of a spoon, stick it to the buttercream, and pull it away. This will create spikes!

7   Pop the cake into the refrigerator for 5 minutes and allow it to set.

8   Use a smooth cloth or paper towel to gently rub against the cake with the palm of your hand to press down the spikes.

9   Arrange broken pieces of brittle, toasted pecans, and dollops of buttercream as you like.

Cupcake Assembly

1   Core each cupcake using an apple corer.

2   Place the buttercream in a piping bag with a 1M tip and pipe a classic swirl on top of each cupcake.

3   Finish with a chunk of pecan brittle on top.

Winter . . . I have a mouthful to say about it, but complaining here won't get me very far.

American Buttercream's extra sweetness will help offset the tart cranberries. Oatmeal crumble is my favourite topping for pies instead of a top crust, and it's great on yogurt or even as a cereal!

This cake brings you winter in a slice: warm chai spice cake filled with a tart cranberry-apple filling and all the oat-topping crunch you can handle.

WINTER:
CRANBERRY-CRUMBLE CAKE

1 batch of **Classic Vanilla Cake batter**, plus 1½ to 2 Tbsp **Chai Spice Mix**, divided evenly into three 8" gooped pans and baked

1 batch of **American Buttercream**

½ cup **Simple Syrup** (not required for cupcakes)

1½ batches of **Fruit Filling** using **cranberries**, **orange** substituted for lemon (zest and juice), sugar increased to ¾ of a cup, and ½ tsp of **cinnamon** added

Baked Oatmeal Crumble (page 195) for decoration

CHAI SPICE MIX
3 Tbsp ground **ginger**

2 Tbsp ground **cinnamon**

1 Tbsp ground **cloves**

1 Tbsp ground **allspice**

1 Tbsp ground **cardamom**

Put all spices in a bowl and mix thoroughly. Place in an airtight container.

Cake Assembly

1   Level the cakes.

2   Spread a small amount of buttercream onto the cake plate so the first layer of cake sticks to it.

3   Layer the cake as follows:

cake—soaked in syrup

buttercream, piped into a dam around the edge (See Damming and Filling, page 15)

one-third of the cranberry filling, filled in the centre

¼ cup of crumble, sprinkled

cake—soaked in syrup

buttercream, piped into a dam around the edge

one-third of the cranberry filling, filled in the centre

¼ cup of crumble, sprinkled

cake—soaked in syrup

4   Place in the refrigerator for 15 to 20 minutes to set before crumb-coating. This will help stabilize the cake and set the buttercream so the layers don't slide apart while finishing.

5   Crumb-coat the cake with a thin layer of buttercream and place back in the refrigerator for 10 to 15 minutes.

BAKED OATMEAL CRUMBLE

You will need 2 cups **quick rolled oats**, 1 cup all-purpose **flour**, ¾ cup packed **brown sugar**, ½ tsp **baking soda**, ¼ tsp **salt**, ¼ tsp ground **cinnamon**, and 1 cup unsalted **butter**, cold and cubed.

Preheat oven to 350°F.

Place the oats, flour, sugar, baking soda, salt, and cinnamon in a bowl and mix well.

Cut the butter into the flour mixture until it is crumbly and has pea-sized butter chunks.

Loosely spread the mixture onto a gooped baking sheet, bake for 18 to 22 minutes until golden brown, remove from the oven, and allow to cool completely before using.

6   Remove from the refrigerator and add the final layer of buttercream. Frost with a rough/rustic finish.

7   Press some of the remaining oatmeal crumble into the frosting at the bottom edge of the cake.

8   Create a wreath of oat crumble around the top of the cake and fill in with the remaining cranberry filling.

Cupcake Assembly

1   Core each cupcake using an apple corer.

2   Place the fruit filling in a piping bag with no tip, and fill each cupcake.

3   Place the buttercream in piping bag with a 1M piping tip, and pipe a rosette onto each cupcake.

4   Top with a pile of oat crumble.

Sticky toffee pudding originally comes to us as a British classic, but it can be traced back to Canadian soldiers in World War Two. No wonder we love it so much!!

The cake is a super-moist sponge made with dates (*I know, dates. Yum!*), and then served with a vanilla custard and loads of warm caramel sauce.

The buttercream replaces the need for the custard or heavy cream that's traditionally served with Sticky Toffee Pudding.

This treat is certainly going to warm you from the inside out. You won't want to leave the house after indulging in a slice of this cake.

1 batch of **Classic Vanilla Cake batter,** with the following adjustments, divided evenly into three 8" gooped pans and baked

Date Mixture substituted for the milk

Packed **brown sugar** substituted for the granulated sugar

½ cup of **molasses** added

1 batch of **Swiss Meringue Buttercream, brown sugar** substituted for the granulated sugar (optional)

½ cup **Simple Syrup** (not required for cupcakes)

Toffee Drip (page 198), for serving

DATE MIXTURE
10½ oz chopped **dates**

1 cup of **water**

WINTER:
STICKY-TOFFEE-PUDDING CAKE

To Make the Date Mixture

1   Cook the dates in the water until the fruit becomes well hydrated and soft. Add more water as needed, ¼ cup at a time.

2   Blend in the food processor until completely smooth. The mixture should be the consistency of soft-serve ice cream.

note If you have leftover date mixture at the end, you can freeze it.

Cake Assembly

1   Level the cakes.

2   Spread a small amount of buttercream onto the cake plate so the first layer of cake sticks to it.

3   Layer the cake as follows:

cake—soaked in syrup

1 cup of buttercream

cake—soaked in syrup

1 cup of buttercream

cake—soaked in syrup

TOFFEE DRIP
*Combine 1 batch of **Caramel Sauce** with 1 Tbsp of **molasses**, 3 Tbsp **heavy cream**, and 2 Tbsp **corn syrup**.*

4   Place in the refrigerator for 15 to 20 minutes before crumb-coating. This will help stabilize the cake and set the buttercream so the layers don't slide apart while finishing.

5   Crumb-coat the cake with a thin layer of buttercream, and, for this cake, it's almost done! This is semi-naked cake—nice and simple.

6   Warm the toffee drip and drizzle it over the cake.

Cupcake Assembly

1   Place the buttercream in a piping bag with a 1A tip, and pipe a blob on top of each cupcake.

2   Heat toffee drip gently in microwave until warm but not hot. Pour a spoonful over the top of each cupcake.

INDEX

A

alcohol
  Beer and Cheese Cake, 153-155
  Cherry Blossom Cake, 51-53
  Christmas Tree Cake, 142-145
  Coffee Crisp Cake, 54-56
  Death-by-Chocolate Cake, 120-123
  Guinness and Baileys Cake, 124-127
  Pink Lemonade Cake, 182-185
  Pumpkin-Pie Cake, 186-189
  Strawberry, White-Chocolate and Pink-Champagne Cake, 113-115
  Terry's Chocolate Orange Cake, 61-62
  Tiramisu Cake, 87-89
Almond Joy Cake, *46*, 48
American Buttercream, 33
apricot jam, 165
Avocado and Coffee Cake, *149*, 150-152

B

bacon
Beer and Cheese Cake, *148*, 153-155
  Maple Bacon Cake, 162-164
Baked Oatmeal Crumble, 195
Baked Streusel, 181
Beer and Cheese Cake, 153-155
Biscuits, Mini, 173
blackberries, 179
Boston-Cream-Pie Cake, *69*, 70-72
Brownies, 120
Burrowing Bunny Cake, *119*, 128-131
buttercreams

American Buttercream, 33
  Swiss Meringue Buttercream, 34
buttermilk substitute, 31

C

Cake-Mix Snickerdoodles, 102
cakes
  decorating techniques, 15-21
  See also chocolate cake; vanilla cake
Campfire S'More Cake, *68*, 73-75
Canada Day Cake, *119*, 132-134
Candied Pecans, 81
Caramel Sauce, 40
  Caramel-Corn Cake, *148*, 156-158
  Dark-Chocolate and Honey Cake, 98-100
  German Chocolate Cake, 80-83
  Pumpkin-Pie Cake, 186-189
  Salted-Caramel Cake, 110-112
  Sticky-Toffee-Pudding Cake, 197-199
  Toffee Drip, 198
  Turtle Cake, 63-65
Caramel-Corn Cake, 156-158
Chai Spice Mix, 194
cheese
  Beer and Cheese Cake, 153-155
  Cinnamon-Roll Cake, 76-79
  Cream Cheese Frosting, 37
  Pastry Cream, 39
  Peach-and-Blackberry-Streusel Cake, 179-181
  Tiramisu Cake, 87-89
Cherry Blossom Cake, *47*, 51-53

Cherry Cream Filling, 52
chocolate
    Chocolate Ganache, 36
    See also chocolate cakes; chocolate decorations; white chocolate
chocolate cakes
    Almond Joy Cake, 48
    Avocado and Coffee Cake, 150-152
    Campfire S'More Cake, 73-75
    Cherry Blossom Cake, 51-53
    Chocolate Cake, 31
    Chocolate, Peanut Butter and Pretzel Cake, *93*, 94-97
    Dark-Chocolate and Honey Cake, 98-100
    Death-by-Chocolate Cake, 120-123
    German Chocolate Cake, 80-83
    Guinness and Baileys Cake, 124-127
    Nanaimo-Bar Cake, 84-86
    Pecan PieCaken, 190-193
    Pumpkin-Pie Cake, 186-189
    Salted-Caramel Cake, 110-112
    Spicy Chocolate Cake, 165-167
    Turtle Cake, 63-65
    Witches' Brew Cake, 138-141
chocolate decorations
    Chocolate Pretzel Bark, 95
    Chocolate Sails, 62
    Chocolate-Dipped Strawberries, 114
    Coloured Chocolate Shards, 134
    Semi-Dipped Pretzels, 96
Christmas Tree Cake, *118*, 142-145
Cinnamon Rolls, Mini, 76
Cinnamon-Roll Cake, *69*, 76-79
citrus fruit. *See* lemons; oranges
Classic Vanilla Cake, 30

coconut
    Almond Joy Cake, 48
    Cherry Blossom Cake, 51-53
    Coconut Caramel Pecan Custard, 80
    Coconut Filling, 48
    Green Shredded Coconut, 131
    Nanaimo-Bar Base, 84
coffee
    Avocado and Coffee Cake, 150-152
    Chocolate Cake, 31-32
    Coffee Crisp Cake, *47*, 54-56
    Tiramisu Cake, 87-89
Coloured Chocolate Shards, 134
conversion table, 25
cookies
    Brownies, 120
    Coffee Crisp Cake, 54-56
    Cookies 'n' Cream Cake, 46, 57-59
    Eggless Cookie Mixture, 101
    ladyfingers, in Tiramisu, 87-89
    Melt-in-Your-Mouth Shortbread Cookies, 102
    Milk-and-Cookies Cake, 101-105
    Peanut-Butter Cookies, 106
Cranberry-Crumble Cake, 194-196
cream cheese
    Beer and Cheese Cake, 153-155
    Cinnamon-Roll Cake, 76-79
    Cream Cheese Frosting, 37
    Peach-and-Blackberry-Streusel Cake, 179-181
Cream Puffs, Mini, 70
crumb-coating, about, 16
cupcakes
    coring and filling, 15
    piping techniques, 19-21

D

damming and filling technique, 15

Dark-Chocolate and Honey Cake, 92, 98-100

Date Mixture, 197

Death-by-Chocolate Cake, *118*, 120-123

dripping technique, 18

E

Eggless Cookie Mixture, 101

F

figs, fresh, 165

fillings

Cherry Cream Filling, 52

Chocolate Ganache, 36

Coconut Caramel Pecan Custard, 80

Coconut Filling, 48

Fruit Filling, 41

Lemon Curd, 38

Pastry Cream, 39

Peanut-Butter-Crunch Filling, 95

See also buttercreams; Caramel Sauce; Fruit Fillings

frostings

techniques, 16-19

See also buttercreams; Chocolate Ganache; cream cheese

fruit fillings

Cranberry-Crumble Cake, 194-196

Fruit Filling, 41

Peach-and-Blackberry-Streusel Cake, 179-181

Peanut Butter and Jam Cake, 106-109

Strawberry Basil Shortcake, 172-175

fruit, fresh

Habanero Jam, 166

Peach-and-Blackberry-Streusel Cake, 179-181

Peanut Butter and Jam Cake, 106-109

Pink Lemonade Cake, 182-185

Spicy Chocolate Cake, 165-167

Strawberry Basil Shortcake, 172-175

Strawberry, White-Chocolate and Pink-Champagne Cake, 113-115

See also fruit fillings

G

Ganache, Chocolate, 36

German Chocolate Cake, *69*, 80-83

Goop, 28

graham crumbs

Graham Crumb Crust, 74

Nanaimo-Bar Base, 84

Green Shredded Coconut, 131

Guinness and Baileys Cake, *119*, 124-127

H

Habanero Jam, 166

Honeycomb Candy, 98

I

Independence Day (US) Cake, 135-137

L

lemons

Lemon Curd, 38

Lemon, Lavender and Rosemary Cake, *171*, 176-178

Lemon, Pepper and Parsley Cake, *148*, 159-161

Pink Lemonade Cake, 182-185
levelling technique, 16

M

Maple Bacon Cake, *149*, 162-164
marshmallows
    Campfire S'More Cake, 73-75
    Marshmallow Spiderweb, 139
    Witches' Brew Cake, 138-141
Melt-in-Your-Mouth Shortbread
    Cookies, 102
Milk-and-Cookies Cake, 92, 101-105
Mini Biscuits, 173
Mini Cinnamon Rolls, 76
Mini Cream Puffs, 70

N

naked cake, about, 16
Nanaimo-Bar Cake, *68*, 84-86
nuts. *See individual nuts*

O

Oatmeal Crumble, Baked, 195
Orange Cake Pops, 138
oranges
    Cranberry-Crumble Cake,
    194-196
    Terry's Chocolate Orange Cake,
    61-62
    Witches' Brew Cake, 138-141

P

Parsley- and Peppercorn-Infused
    Milk, 159
Pastry Cream, 39
Peach-and-Blackberry-Streusel
    Cake, *170*, 179-181
peanuts/peanut butter
    Cherry Blossom Cake, 51-53

Chocolate, Peanut Butter and
    Pretzel Cake, 94-97
Peanut Butter and Jam Cake, *93*,
    106-109
Peanut-Butter-Crunch Filling, 95
pears, 165-166
pecans
    Candied Pecans, 81
    Coconut Caramel Pecan Custard,
    80
    Pecan Pie, 190
    Pecan PieCaken, *171*, 190-193
    Toasted Pecan Brittle, 191
    Turtle Cake, 63-65
pepper
    Lemon, Pepper and Parsley Cake,
    159-161
petal piping, 20
Pink Drip, 184
Pink Lemonade Cake, *171*, 182-185
piping techniques, 19
pretzels
    Chocolate, Peanut Butter and
    Pretzel Cake, 94-97
    Pretzel Trees, 144
    Semi-Dipped Pretzels, 96
Pumpkin-Pie Cake, *171*, 186-189

R

raspberries
    Pink Lemonade Cake, 182-185
rosette piping, 19

S

Salted-Caramel Cake, 92, 110-112
scoop table, 25
semi-naked cake, about, 17
shortbread cookies, 102

Simple Syrup, 16, 29
Spicy Chocolate Cake, *149*, 165-167
spider, 141
Spiderwebs, Marshmallow, 139
Sticky-Toffee-Pudding Cake, *170*, 197-199
strawberries
    Peanut Butter and Jam Cake, 106-109
    Strawberry Basil Shortcake, *170*, 172-175
    Strawberry, White-Chocolate and Pink-Champagne Cake, *92*, 113-115
streusel, 181
Swiss Meringue Buttercream, 34

T

tempering, 39
Terry's Chocolate Orange Cake, 47, 61-62
Tiramisu Cake, *68*, 87-89
Toasted Pecan Brittle, 191
Toffee Drip, 198
tools, 24
torting technique, 16
Turtle Cake, *46*, 63-65

V

vanilla cakes
    Beer and Cheese Cake, 153-155
    Boston-Cream-Pie Cake, 70-72
    Burrowing Bunny Cake, 128-131
    Canada Day Cake, 132-134
    Caramel-Corn Cake, 156-158
    Chocolate, Peanut Butter and Pretzel Cake, 94-97
    Christmas Tree Cake, 142-145
    Cinnamon-Roll Cake, 76-79
    Classic Vanilla Cake, 30

Coffee Crisp Cake, 54-56
Cookies 'n' Cream Cake, 57-59
Cranberry-Crumble Cake, 194-196
Independence Day (US) Cake, 135-137
Lemon, Lavender and Rosemary Cake, 176-178
Lemon, Pepper and Parsley Cake, 159-161
Maple Bacon Cake, 162-164
Milk-and-Cookies Cake, 101-105
Peach-and-Blackberry-Streusel Cake, 179-181
Peanut Butter and Jam Cake, 106-109
Pink Lemonade Cake, 182-185
Sticky-Toffee-Pudding Cake, 197-199
Strawberry Basil Shortcake, 172-175
Strawberry, White-Chocolate and Pink-Champagne Cake, 113-115
Terry's Chocolate Orange Cake, 61-62
Tiramisu Cake, 87-89

W

walnuts
    Nanaimo-Bar Base, 84
white chocolate
    Chocolate Ganache, 36
    Strawberry, White-Chocolate and Pink-Champagne Cake, 113-115
    Witches' Brew Cake, *119*, 138-141

AARON MCINNIS owns the custom cake studio Happy Belly Cakery and the blog *Man versus Cake*. A certified nutritionist, Aaron is also a father of three boys—he believes in deconstructing the idea that men belong under a car or up a ladder and that fancy baking is for women. As a participant in the Food Network's *Spring Baking Championship*, Aaron placed fifth out of ten contestants, stretching his imagination and creativity to new dimensions. He competed in *Christmas Cookie Challenge* (season 2, episode 4) and was crowned winner and Christmas Cookie Champion. He also participated in *Winner Cake All*. He is an occasional contributor to *American Cake Decorating*. Aaron is passionate about his work, seeking every opportunity to better the world through cake and to empower cakers, bakers, and sweet-treat makers globally.